"Every community developing a strategy to put their schools in the top tier will want to use this book as a guide."
r University Fellow, and former Education

"Valuable ... repreneurship in education ... anyone concerned with our nation's future." —*Tulsa World*

"A highly readable book that articulates clearly some of the complex factors affecting schools."
—Floretta Dukes McKenzie, former deputy commissioner of the Department of Education and former Washington, D.C., Superintendent of Schools

"Offers valuable lessons . . . and presents the essence of the corporate vision of reform in U.S. public education."
—*Booklist*

"With vivid examples, the authors spell out how to create dynamic schools worthy of our children. There are lessons here for anyone who cares about reforming public education."
—Thomas H. Kean, President, Drew University and former governor of New Jersey

"Heartening . . . makes an eloquent plea for change if future generations are to meet the demands of the 21st century."
—*Kirkus Reviews*

"To every teacher, principal, and business person in America, I say, 'Read it! Put its lessons to work for you. And your schools will reclaim their legacy too.'"
—John A. Murphy, Superintendent of Charlotte-Mecklenburg Schools

LOUIS V. GERSTNER, JR., formerly chairman and CEO of RJR Nabisco, is now chairman and CEO of IBM. ROGER D. SEMERAD, formerly senior vice president of RJR Nabisco, is treasurer of the New American Schools Development Corporation. DENIS PHILIP DOYLE, a major figure in the education policy debate, is the author of numerous books and articles and a senior fellow at the Hudson Institute. WILLIAM B. JOHNSTON is an executive vice president at Burson-Marsteller and a senior fellow at the Hudson Institute.

Reinventing Education

Entrepreneurship in America's Public Schools

Louis V. Gerstner, Jr., Roger D. Semerad, Denis Philip Doyle, and William B. Johnston

A PLUME BOOK

PLUME
Published by the Penguin Group
Penguin Books USA Inc., 375 Hudson Street, New York, New York 10014, U.S.A.
Penguin Books Ltd, 27 Wrights Lane, London W8 5TZ, England
Penguin Books Australia Ltd, Ringwood, Victoria, Australia
Penguin Books Canada Ltd, 10 Alcorn Avenue, Toronto, Ontario, Canada M4V 3B2
Penguin Books (N.Z.) Ltd, 182–190 Wairau Road, Auckland 10, New Zealand

Penguin Books Ltd, Registered Offices: Harmondsworth, Middlesex, England

Published by Plume, an imprint of Dutton Signet,
a division of Penguin Books USA Inc.
Previously published in a Dutton edition.

First Plume Printing, May, 1995
10 9 8 7 6 5 4 3 2 1

The Library of Congress has catalogued the Dutton edition as follows:

Reinventing education : entrepreneurship in America's public schools /
    by Louis V. Gerstner, Jr. . . . [et al.].
        p.   cm.
    ISBN 0-525-93749-8 (hc.)
    ISBN 0-452-27145-2 (pbk.)
    1. Public schools—United States. 2. School management and
organization—United States. 3. Entrepreneurship—United States.
4. Educational changes—United States. I. Gerstner, Louis V.
LA217.2.R45   1994
371'.01'0973—dc20   93–39205
                                                       CIP

Printed in the United States of America
Designed by Eve L. Kirch

*To the teachers, principals, and students
of the Next Century Schools program, who are changing
the future for America's children.*

CONTENTS

Foreword

by Louis V. Gerstner, Jr.

Before becoming CEO and Chairman of IBM, I had been involved in educational reform for more than twenty years, first at American Express and then at RJR Nabisco. At American Express, my work in education began when I had the opportunity to establish the National Academy Foundation. This program seeks to provide inner-city high school students with the educational tools they need to succeed in the job market. The move to RJR Nabisco provided the opportunity to design from scratch a major education program that incorporated all of my views on how business can help at the school level to achieve success. This program, the RJR Nabisco Next Century Schools program, is the wellspring for the ideas contained in this book.

During my tenure at IBM, I have intensified my commitment to school reform. I do this through my service as vice chair of the New American Schools Development Corporation (NASDC), an effort to bring to scale the efforts of single-school reform in demonstration districts and states across the country. But most important, I have pursued my interest in education by putting the weight of IBM's philanthropic program behind the reform of our nation's schools.

IBM's new five-year initiative in K–12 education is also

called Reinventing Education. It is designed to use the power of technology as a tool to achieve meaningful and lasting school reform in the way teachers educate children and in the way our school districts are managed and operated. In partnership with whole school districts, we intend to alter the organization of our systems and districts so that schools such as the Next Century Schools can become the norm, not the exception.

Our first such partnership in Charlotte, North Carolina, announced in September 1994, called for the construction of an Education Village consisting of four "schools of the future." These schools will serve as a hub for changes in teacher training throughout the district. They will operate like teaching hospitals, helping all the teachers in this district to learn new skills and meet higher standards. But the schools will have radically changed systems for everything from testing and evaluating students to the governance structure of the system.

Incredibly, we still hear from learned professionals that there is no problem with how we educate our children. If you are an employer, you do not need Pollyannaish opinions that dispute most of today's dismal data. You know that most young applicants are not qualified to do today's more intellectually demanding jobs, let alone tomorrow's. Businesspeople and politicians talk glibly about the need for America to become "more competitive" in the international economy of the next century. But it is unrealistic to believe we can do this without significantly improving our public schools.

My interest in education reform is not just philanthropic: It is fueled by intense anger and frustration. My co-authors and I are dismayed by the slowness and indifference our country brings to the crisis in public-education reform. We live in a time when nearly all of our institutions, including

American industry, labor unions, churches, and government, are struggling to adapt to the changes of the late twentieth century. Yet in the institution where progress is arguably most critical—education—it is most lacking. Where are our passion and commitment to our most precious asset, our children? Where are our collective will and determination to give our children what they deserve and need—high-quality education?

This book largely focuses on my experiences with the Next Century Schools program, experiences that have shaped the design and focus of IBM's new initiative. Why Next Century Schools? Because too often we find our schools resistant to change and rooted, not in the current century, but in the last. In fact, I often point out that if an American were put in a time capsule in 1895 and it was opened 100 years later, there would be few things in American life that person would recognize; transportation, communications, and virtually every facet of daily life would have changed. The only American enterprise with which our latter-day Rip Van Winkle would be comfortable is our schools, since they are remarkably similar to the schools we had before the Spanish-American War.

The Next Century Schools program was designed to improve the academic performance of students, and our vehicle was grants to "individual schools." The first grant awards were made in April 1990, and the last group of three-year awards was made in April 1992. Over this time, the program committed nearly $30 million to 42 schools.

We made grants to the teachers and principals themselves, the men and women in the front lines who had direct responsibility for educating children. School districts were not permitted to take overhead or siphon off regular funds once the grants were made. And although the Foundation was pleased if other indicators of student behavior or community satisfaction improved, student performance was the target. That is what school is about. A school's "value added" is knowledge.

In making these grants, we were looking for education "entrepreneurs," men and women who were risk-takers, who were prepared to design and put in place their own innovative and daring programs. Central to the award process was the conviction that the only programs that would work were those that committed themselves to real change at the building level.

The result was a wide variety of innovations: extended-day and year-round programs in Park View Elementary School in Mooresville, North Carolina; heavy parental involvement, including parenting programs, in Ortega Elementary School in Austin, Texas; enhanced curricular offerings, both to motivate students and to raise standards, in Piscataquis Community High, Guilford, Maine; greater utilization of technology to increase education productivity in Rappahannock Elementary School, Sperryville, Virginia; the creation of schools near the parents' place of work in Winston-Salem, North Carolina, at the Downtown School; and new groupings of students and longer time with the same teachers in New Stanley Elementary in Kansas City, Kansas.

Most important was the Foundation's conviction that no idea was off limits. As the Next Century Schools grant announcement said: "The most promising way to think about Next Century Schools is to think as an entrepreneur does— 'What would I do if I could do anything I wanted, subject only to one constraint: meeting customer requirements?' "

We sought out individuals who were ready to construct new solutions to educational problems, and provided them with the financing to try to realize their dreams. We did not dictate or demand any specific types of programs or reforms. We viewed ourselves as venture capitalists, backing those educators who came to us with bold ideas and pragmatic plans.

We found resourceful teachers, principals, and parents who believed that together they could overcome the stifling culture of the education bureaucracy and create new learning environments that would produce more qualified students. Like all venture capitalists, we knew some of these bold ideas would fail. In fact, we funded two schools that were never able to execute their ideas and others that put their plans in place, only to learn they made little difference in student performance. But the great majority of Next Century Schools have made a difference—transforming, in various ways, the operation of their schools and improving the skills and knowledge of their pupils.

This book tells their story. It is a story of a set of schools with extraordinary leadership that have been called into existence by acts of will and commitment. Every community in America must have good schools if we are to meet the future with confidence. But to do that will require more than creating models; it will involve the political will to change all schools.

The importance of transforming America's schools has now been widely recognized, from the White House, which has championed passage of the Goals 2000 legislation, to the proverbial man in the street. While Goals 2000 is an important step, it is only an initial step; far more dramatic action is needed by the national government, states, and local school districts. However, resistance from teachers, administrators, parents, and school board members, to even the slightest change, is far too prevalent. Many Next Century Schools initially encountered fierce resistance to their bold ideas. And in states and school districts all across the country, structural changes have met with concerted opposition from special interests. Indeed, in one Next Century Schools jurisdiction where student performance ranked very low, an individual ran for the school board promising resistance to change. He won.

Let me emphasize one thing: I do not believe the Next Century Schools model is the only answer to the problems of American schools. In fact, we have learned that the existence of a number of schools operating on the cutting edge of school reform does not necessarily lead to replication. In fact, sometimes the mere existence of these schools becomes a threat or creates an excuse not to change.

It is important to recognize that the current school system was designed over 150 years ago and supported this nation's extraordinarily successful industrial era very well. The problem is not with the concept but with the fact that in its current highly regulated and process-oriented form, mass public education no longer works. It no longer adequately prepares young people for the work world, a world that has changed dramatically and will change even more in the years ahead. What we teach, how we teach it, and what we expect from students and teachers must change, and change rapidly, if we are to succeed in the twenty-first century.

My co-authors and I wrote *Reinventing Education* for parents, teachers and administrators, businessmen and women, state legislators, state superintendents, school board members, and especially for students. It is a book for any reader with an interest in education or for anyone seeking solutions and ideas that can be applied at the state and local level.

We did not write this book to further discuss problems with educational performance or to assign blame. We, as adults, are all to blame. We must overcome both our natural loyalty to our children's accomplishments and our schools' inability to recognize that too few of our graduates have mastered even the minimum knowledge required in a much more competitive world. This threat to all Americans is frightening. But it is one that we have both the resources and the knowledge to overcome.

We felt it important to share the encouraging experiences of dedicated educators who are showing the way now. I should also point out that with every successful reform effort—and there are many across America—there are doubters, naysayers, and critics who discount change. These opponents believe that, either by active resistance or benign neglect, change will be temporary. They make excuses for the current system and resist change actively.

We believe, however, that the future of the great American experiment in self-government is at stake. It is that dramatic and that simple. Jefferson noted that "if a nation expects to be ignorant and free, . . . it expects what never was and never will be." A democracy can exist only if there is a climate of civic virtue and an educated citizenry. If our people's educational levels decline, our economy will no doubt suffer, but democracy itself will be the first casualty.

Our economic abundance, once the envy of the world, cannot continue unless all Americans are well educated. We cannot leave anyone out—not just for reasons of morality and decency, though they are important, but for reasons of social cohesion and even survival. No society can be so wealthy as to afford poverty in its midst. Education in the modern economy is the engine of growth and prosperity. We look to an educated workforce not to benefit just business but to benefit all Americans.

The Chinese character for *crisis* is made up of two characters, one for *danger,* the other for *opportunity.* This book is about opportunity. Our schools are in trouble, to be sure, yet we know enough to act. The unofficial battle cry of the Next Century Schools program was, "No more prizes for predicting rain: prizes only for building arks." We were convinced when we set up the program—as we still are—that now is the time for action. The narrative that follows provides a blueprint for "arks," vessels that will carry us successfully into the twenty-first century. It is based, not on wishful thinking, but on experience; not on dreams, but on solid accomplishment.

This book, then, has one goal: to advance solutions. The battle to reinvent America's schools is not going to be won by generals, least of all by armchair generals. It will be won schoolroom by schoolroom, school building by school building, and school district by school district, state by state. An image we have used in describing the process is house-to-house combat, and that only slightly exaggerates the nature of the process. We hope you will join us in this important undertaking to protect America's future.

CHAPTER 1

Change in a Changing World: Schools for the Next Century

Most Americans, when asked, say they want their children to know more than they do, and are appalled by the prospect that the next generation will know less. Yet so long as today's professional norms and beliefs hold sway, so long as they shape what actually occurs in the classroom, that is precisely the future that awaits our children.

—Chester E. Finn, Jr.

Americans, more than the citizens of any other nation, are wedded to change. As a nation of immigrants, Americans have prospered because they have broken with the past. Our nation was born in revolution, and we must reinvent our experiment with self-government every generation. So too our culture and social order. In attempting to realize our ideal of equality, we have struggled constantly to improve opportunities for those who are not born to wealth or social position. Our economic vitality is also the product of unending change, not only of product cycles and manufacturing transformations, but new ideas and new processes that replace the past as they create the future.

The secret of American economic and political vitality is our greatest social invention: mass education, and the commitment to educate all our citizens at public expense. However, ironically, this one most vital area of our national life—public education—has not undergone the same process of revitalizing change. In our economic and social life we expect change, but in the public schools we have clung tenaciously to the ideas and techniques of earlier decades and even previous centuries. In many ways the public school classroom of today is indistinguishable from the classrooms

3

of our parents and grandparents: A teacher stands in front of twenty to thirty children for seven hours per day, imparting a version of the knowledge contained in fraying textbooks and dog-eared workbooks. A principal with little authority runs the school as part of a large, hierarchical system. Schools look the most like industrial plants from a vanished era. A time traveler from 1942 or perhaps even one from 1892 would easily recognize yesterday's traditions in today's schools.

Yet, even a thumbnail sketch of America over the past five decades reveals dramatic changes: Television and video games now dominate children's attention and time; epidemics of drug use and sexual activity have become routine in high schools; the number of immigrants entering the country and the public schools has doubled; twice as many mothers work outside the home; the number of people jailed for serious crimes has tripled; urban public schools have been virtually abandoned by whites; the number of births to unmarried women has risen by more than 700 percent to one million annually; and computers have revolutionized information storage and communications.

Through these astonishing changes in demography, social conditions, technology, and economics, the schools have stayed basically the same. This immutability in the face of overwhelming change is not surprising. Change is liberating but daunting. It is also creative yet nerve-wracking. Few individuals or institutions welcome change, unless it becomes necessary. Today, in our public schools, it is most certainly necessary.

Why is the need for change so urgent? The rising tide of dismal education reports is by now familiar to most Americans. American students are falling behind. They are doing worse today than students have done historically; our children are performing much worse than children from nations with whom they compete internationally. In mathematics and science, for example, American high schoolers come in last or next to last in virtually every international measure. SAT scores have fallen to historic lows. Trying not to sound too grim about the news regarding declining SAT scores, Don Stewart, president of the College Board (the SAT sponsor), says these scores reflect "a disturbing pattern of educational disparity in academic preparation." Fallen SAT scores are not just a symbol. As Stewart observes, "we could evolve into a nation divided between a small . . . elite and an underclass of students academically ill-prepared for the demands of college or the workplace."

In some respects we already have. Fifty years ago, the major cities were predominantly white and working class. Today they are nonwhite and poor. Indeed, fifty years ago our great cities were the site of great public schools. A few such schools remain, but their numbers are declining. Washington, D.C., offers a vivid example: With 15,500 youngsters in public high schools, only 381 are white. The remaining students are overwhelmingly "poor" students—they exhibit distressingly low levels of academic accomplishment. This contrast is driven home by the extraordinary distribution of Preliminary Scholastic Aptitude Test (PSAT) scores in Washington. Students take the PSAT in their junior year, a year before the SAT, as a trial run. The PSAT scores are also used to determine eligibility for Merit Scholarships. Merit Scholarships are available in every jurisdiction in the U.S. and are apportioned on the basis of population; as a consequence, cut-off scores differ state-by-state. The range between the highest scoring and lowest scoring states is typically more than twenty points, or a 10 percent difference between Mississippi, among the lowest scoring states, and

5

Washington, D.C., the highest scoring. How is it possible that Washington, D.C., has the highest PSAT scores in the nation when the students in its public schools are among the least successful? Each year Washington records about seventy-five Merit Finalists and Semifinalists—but seventy to seventy-two are students in private schools, while only three or fewer are in public schools.

The public schools in Washington, D.C., and countless other big cities have become schools of last resort, peopled by families without the resources to move their children to private schools or suburban public schools. The most dismal vision of a two-class society is becoming a reality in much of the nation's urban public schools.

The problems of school failure are not restricted to the poor and the dispossessed, of course, though it is clear they suffer the most. Look, for example, at what has been happening in the larger society. In important respects, the nation as a whole has slipped backward. The 1991 SAT scores were among the worst in history: The SAT verbal score has never been lower and the SAT math slipped to its lowest point since 1980. One portion of the SAT, the Test of Standard Written English (TSWE), is particularly alarming. As the College Board analysis noted, "after seven years of gains or holding steady, three years of consecutive decline brought the TSWE score to an all-time low." In a season of grim education news, the TSWE's plunge to its lowest levels in history is even more sobering than the SAT decline.

A student's command of "standard written English" is a measurement of what a student has learned—not aptitude, not ability, but knowledge and proficiency. The capacity to use standard English—or standard Japanese or Farsi or French—is neither inborn nor innate. Mastery of a particular language, and its rules and conventions, is acquired the

6

old-fashioned way: by hard work. The fall in the TSWE can be explained in only one way: the failure of schools to invest enough time and effort to train young people to communicate clearly in writing, and the failure of students to invest enough time and effort to learn.

Despite this evidence of absolute decline in student performance, some have argued that the issue is not so much that our schools are doing a worse job of preparing today's students, but simply that they are not doing any better. In this view, the problem is that society and the modern economy are demanding more of schools. While techniques, curricula, and performance have not changed much since World War II, job-skill requirements have escalated steadily.

A 1991 Department of Education report concluded that student performance had hardly changed at all in twenty years. The National Assessment of Educational Progress (NAEP) benchmark, which is based on a standardized test administered to a large sample of American students in grades four, eight, and twelve, is probably the best single summary of U.S. educational performance. It concludes that while minority students have made some progress over the last two decades, most students have not. More worrisome, the absolute levels of achievement are dismal: Only 1 percent of twelfth-graders can write a satisfactory paragraph summarizing the material in a sports article.

Other evidence reinforces the notion that American education is not measuring up. Despite repeated campaigns by educators and others, more than 25 percent of the young people in virtually every large American city leave high school without graduating. For these drop-outs, and those who stay on but learn little, America has nothing to offer. As jobs have become more complex and skill needs have risen, the opportunities for the least educated have all but vanished.

Perhaps most dispiriting of all is the attempt by some educators to claim that there is nothing wrong with American education, but there is something wrong with the dismal reports about it. In 1991, Gerald Bracey, a one-time National Education Association staff member writing in the nation's leading education journal, the *Phi Delta Kappan,* argued that all was well with American education; the bad news was the work of pessimists and complainers. Within two weeks, the *Washington Post* trumpeted this good news on Page One. Incredibly, some analysts and interest-group representatives appear to think that the problem can be simply wished away.

Ask any business leader who competes in the global economy. What is it like to be up against well-educated workforces? What does it do to your competitive position when the Japanese graduate 96 percent of their seventeen-year-olds, compared to America's graduation rate of 72 percent? What does it mean that Japanese youngsters have attended school for 243 days a year for thirteen years, while their American counterparts have gone only 180 days, on average? Does that give their workforce a competitive edge? Of course it does. All the Pollyannas in the world cannot disguise the fact that our schools, and therefore our nation, are in deep trouble.

It is important to stress that the trouble we find ourselves in is not a business problem. America does not need more vocational training, or a more docile and pliant workforce. To the contrary, the problem is that too many American youngsters are no longer able to take their place with the best and brightest in the world. As a consequence, their standard of living will slip, their sense of accomplishment will be diminished, and their role as productive citizens and workers will be diminished as well.

The problem is stark; for as far as we can see into the future—certainly during the next ten years—the U.S. economy will create virtually no new jobs for those who lack basic skills. Put simply, it takes more human capital to earn a decent living today, to make a real contribution to a business, or for a firm to make a world-competitive product. As a result, we are paying our well-educated people more, and our uneducated people relatively less. We are falling behind our competitors in some industries, and we are not improving our economic well-being as much as we could. This is a vast economic waste, a tragedy for our society, and a personal hardship for millions.

Consider, for example, a story told by Admiral Watkins, Secretary of Energy under President George Bush. A World War II cruiser had a complement of about 1,700 sailors, each averaging an eighth-grade education. The modern battle cruiser has a crew of 700, each with an average education of two years beyond high school. In terms of both social and individual "investment" in human capital, the difference is striking; each modern crew member has, on average, attended school six years more than the World War II counterpart. Even though individuals must be much better educated to serve on a modern cruiser, the efficiency gains of reduced crew sizes—because of modern computerization—represent an enormous social cost/benefit improvement.

This example is a metaphor for the modern economy as a whole, and is repeated in industry after industry. Motorola, IBM, Xerox, and many others have had nearly identical experiences in modernizing plant and work processes. As electronics replace electromechanical machinery, productivity skyrockets. Workers can perform new tasks in new settings with new equipment. But the transition is difficult, even impossible, if the employee is not educated. The truth is that the modern firm cannot train if the school has not educated.

In case after case, American industry has discovered that the skills of the past are not even marginally adequate for the present. When Motorola decided to "make it in America," they had not only to retrain but to reeducate many members of their workforce. Many of the dedicated men and women who had worked on the old assembly lines could not make the transition to the electronic era without massive remedial education. They could not read the manuals, could not read the keyboards or the screens, and they could not make the shift to the modern, high-performance corporation.

A vivid example is found in the production of textiles, made all the more vivid because the power loom laid the foundation for the industrial revolution two hundred years ago. Like the original waterpowered loom, the modern electromechanical power loom could be operated successfully by semiliterate workers who were bright, inventive, and enterprising. Even an eighth-grade drop-out could understand the mechanical movements and connections of complex machinery so long as they were visible. But replace the old loom with computer-guided processes and the eighth-grade drop-out is simply unable to meet the new requirements. Unable to read and understand the documentation that renders the computer's software comprehensible, the loom operator is unable to operate the loom. Indeed, the job is no longer "loom operator"; the computer is the "loom operator." The new job is "troubleshooter."

This pattern is not unique to textiles; it is true in every industry, from computer manufacturing and assembly, to health care and packaged-goods manufacturing. Just as the original industrial revolution "dumbed-down" work, making

10

it simple and less complex, the modern technology-based manufacturing process "smartens up" work, requiring more skilled workers. There is little need to spend more time reanalyzing this problem, or wringing our hands over it. The remedy is straightforward: more and better education.

How can our public schools provide more and better education? In order to revitalize our schools, we must define more clearly why these institutions are failing and what we can do to fix them. How is it that American public schools, once the envy of the world, have fallen into such disrepute? Has there been a conspiracy to undermine the nation's well-being? One might think so after reading the language of reform reports such as *A Nation at Risk,* which asserted in 1983 that "if an unfriendly foreign power had imposed our schools upon us we would have regarded it as an act of war."

Despite the striking rhetoric, the explanations for our schools' weaknesses are not sinister. There was no conspiracy; there is no villain in this story. This is not the work of malign people or forces. It is not exclusively the product of excessive union demands or inept management.

Rather it is that schools as institutions have lacked the mechanism for self-renewal. Unlike businesses that are periodically forced to respond to new technologies, new demands from their markets, or the obsolescence of products, no external forces have demanded that schools change. Schools have been able to ignore the revolutionary possibilities of technology, to keep the same hierarchical organizational structure, to preserve traditional rules governing the numbers of students in each class and type of school, and to stick with the traditional curriculum and teaching styles used throughout this century. The schools have not gotten worse, they have simply not changed for the better.

Nowhere is this better illustrated than in the schools' use

of new technologies. In no other part of the economy is the absence of technology so startling and so complete. Even our oldest, most enduring and traditional institutions— churches, mosques, and synagogues—use technology more inventively and more effectively than schools. In the economy as a whole, including private-sector "teaching and learning services," technology reins supreme. Put most vividly and simply, the schools of the present are like a nineteenth-century farm: labor-intensive and low-tech. Like farms before tractors and fertilizer, before milking machines and hybrid-seed corn, the school comprises a low-capital, low-productivity system. Despite the invention of a staggering array of new information tools that store and communicate knowledge, and that entertain, challenge, and extend the power of their users, schools transmit information as they have since Gutenberg. Indeed, the only technologies that have made much headway in schools are the most primitive and intrusive, like the public address systems for school-wide announcements, which are a menace in most settings because they encourage mindless interruptions. When schools do employ technology, they treat it most often as an add-on or extra. Computers are typically in a separate lab, to which students are periodically sent. The software they use most often has little or no relation to the curriculum in the textbooks or other materials. In most schools technology is treated like a car radio; it has no effect on performance, no effect on handling. It is an extra that provides pleasure, amusement, and occasional information. There is, to be sure, in some schools the promise of higher technology; a faint sense that things can and should be different. But this is the exception, not the norm.

No term has gained wider currency in education, or is more poorly understood, than *restructuring*. In the business world, restructuring has a reasonably clear meaning—it is the sum total of the painful processes of totally changing the way in which business is transacted, from rethinking the goals and purposes of the organization to deploying the traditional factors of production, labor, and capital. Restructuring in a business context means transformation, from top to bottom. Restructuring is not a matter of changing titles or production runs, though it usually involves both. Restructuring requires fundamental changes in the relationships within an organization and between the organization and its customers.

As a consequence, restructuring is not a process entered into lightly or unadvisedly. In fact, it cannot occur except under conditions of the utmost urgency. Restructuring in the business world occurs (when it occurs at all) because it must. Corporations restructure because if they do not periodically reorient themselves to the changes in the marketplace, they will go bankrupt. Markets, with their impersonal and amoral demands, implacably force competitive institutions to change. Goods and services that have no customers go begging. They are not foisted upon unwilling members of the public, as public-sector services are. It is not an accident that there are no dreadful schools in the private sector; there are no customers for dreadful schools. No one will voluntarily patronize them.

Think, for example, of the differences between America's widely criticized public elementary and secondary schools, and its widely envied system of higher education. The most important reason behind the dramatic differences in these two systems is the way they are organized, and the environment in which they must operate. Public elementary and secondary schools are a protected monopoly, owned and operated by government and enjoying captive clienteles; col-

13

leges and universities, public and private, by way of contrast, must compete for students. The difference is striking, because one set of institutions must respond to its clients, another is free to ignore them. Public schools that are attentive to the demands of their clients, are so because they are moved to be, not because they must be. Their penalty for ignoring their clients is public complaints and criticism, not closure. They may have bad reputations, but they need not change their behavior or close their doors.

Alone among the developed nations, American higher education exists in a market of willing buyers and willing sellers. Unlike other developed nations where higher education is a government monopoly, American colleges and universities must recruit their students. And in this harsh competitive environment, American higher education has thrived. Alone among the world's systems of higher education, the U.S. enrolls two-thirds of its high school graduates and more than 400,000 students from other nations in higher education. Unlike other systems of higher education, the U.S. has developed an astounding array of educational institutions, from community colleges providing technically skilled people to local employers, to great research universities pursuing the frontiers of knowledge.

This ability to attract students, to develop new education missions, and to satisfy a constantly changing variety of education customers results from having to operate in a market system, and being forced to restructure, meet change, or fold. No one in higher education, not the college president, not the mail-room clerk, not the trustees, not the graduates, and certainly not the professors, enters into restructuring without misgivings and anxiety. Restructuring would not be attempted if it were not essential. But markets force change: periodic, painful restructuring. In the public schools, no unseen, amoral hand forces restructuring. The public schools have been able to avoid the frustrating, frightening, disorienting ordeal of change.

From a business perspective, then, the central problem for American public schools is that they have not been forced to continuously adapt themselves to the changes in their students and the demands of society and the economy. Operating outside the market, they have been insulated from the necessity to change.

A business perspective not only sheds light on the nature of the problem, it suggests strategies for a solution. The techniques and disciplines of business have much to offer in the field of education. Noneducators cannot claim to be able to do a better job in the classroom than teachers, or to do a better job of running schools than principals. But the strategies that businesses have developed to deal with change, and to manage large and small organizations, have a direct bearing on schools. Management lessons have been proven again and again in the last several decades. They are the subject of countless business school textbooks, magazine articles, and seminars. But they are missing from the language and practice of American public education. Simple organizational ideas like listening to customers, decentralized decision-making, measuring performance, and continuous improvement are notable by their absence in public schools. These ideas and techniques have had undeniable power in the business and nonprofit worlds, and when applied to schools, they can lead to dramatic results. The issue is not just making schools more businesslike; rather, it is to run schools like other successful organizations. Just as businesses are results-oriented, schools must also be. It is time for results in education.

CHAPTER 2

The Dynamism of the Market

Accountability and responsiveness in public education cannot be legislated, regulated or achieved by fiat or good intentions alone. They require both incentives and disincentives. The system that best meets these objectives fairly, efficiently and rapidly is a market system.

—*Investing in Our Children: Business and the Public Schools*
Committee for Economic Development

This is a book about public schools—and their last, best chance to save themselves. They must reinvent themselves in order to survive. The "discipline of the market" provides the key. Schools cannot be "regulated" back into good health; regulation, itself, is a large part of the problem. The history of public schools—including reform and renewal—is the story of regulation run amok, good intentions that produce no good end. At least over the long haul. Because the history of regulation is re-regulation, an endless cycle of reforming the preceding reform.

The reason is not hard to fathom. The public policy tool kit contains blunt instruments only: laws, rules, regulations. Governors, state legislators, county commissioners, and school board members are all constrained by the same limitations: Instead of incentives to perform or rewards for success, the policymaker issues orders to bureaucrats. To be sure, statutes and regulations are necessary and proper, but they are tools designed to prevent abuse, not to stimulate superior performance.

Public institutions that fail to perform are subject to regulatory review and control; budgets can be juggled and adjusted; in the event of dismal performance, civil servants can be disciplined, even fired. But there are almost no rewards for success and few penalties for poor performance. A public institution that slides may do so indefinitely without corrective action being taken.

Contrast public institutions to institutions that are subject to market forces. Markets reward success and punish failure in the private, for-profit sector; but they also work in the not-for-profit world. Museums, theaters, colleges, universities, zoos, or libraries that fail to draw patrons are "disciplined" by market forces; clients, customers, students, or patrons who withhold their patronage send a strong message.

To see the impact of "market" forces on public institutions, contrast public schools of choice to neighborhood assignment schools. Choice schools—typically magnet schools, which are organized by academic theme or emphasis—must meet customer requirements to "stay in business." And they do. Study after study reveals what common sense already knows: Schools that are subject to market discipline, even of a moderate kind, are more responsive, more effective, and more popular than schools that are not. As the prestigious Committee for Economic Development said in its pathbreaking study, *Investing in Our Children: Business and the Public Schools:*

> Most students are assigned to schools by accidents of geography.... It is no wonder that schools, lacking competition, exhibit many of the characteristics of monopolies. As a public sector activity, schools will never be subject to the full play of the market. Nevertheless, we believe that certain market incentives and disincentives can and should be introduced into public schooling. For example, regional or even statewide open-enrollment systems would make it possible ...

to choose from among a wide variety of public schools. Such freedom of choice would reward schools that meet the educational objectives of the families that select them and send a message to those schools that are bypassed.

The lesson is clear: To succeed, public schools must be "deregulated." They must be free to meet their objectives. They must be held to high standards, but those standards must be of a special kind: performance standards. Schools must meet the test any high-performance organization must meet: results. And results are not achieved by bureaucratic regulation. They are achieved by meeting customer requirement by rewards for success and penalties for failure. Market discipline is the key, the ultimate form of accountability.

The Lessons of the Market

The lessons of the market are overwhelmingly important. The essence of the market is the active interplay of supply and demand: "choice," both on the part of suppliers and consumers. Unfortunately, however, the word *choice* has acquired much political baggage over the past decade, symbolizing both the bitter fight over abortion and the bitter fight in the education world about public aid for religious schools. But the real meaning of *choice* in education is to harness the most powerful aspect of the market, the voluntary coming together of willing buyers and sellers. Just as we choose our elected officials, our houses of worship, the stores and shops we patronize, so too, should we be able to select our schools. It is in the best interest of the public at large and the schools themselves. Schools subject to market forces are healthier institutions, for they reap rewards as well as run risks. Indeed, it is because they are willing to run risks that they reap rewards.

The significance of selecting among public schools has not been lost on the nation's governors. In *Time for Results: The Governors' 1991 Report on Education,* prepared by the National Governors' Association, the governors said:

> There is nothing more basic to education and its ability to bring our children into the 21st century than choice. Given a choice in public education, we believe parents will play a stronger role in our schools. Innovative programs will spring to life. Parents and the whole community will become more deeply involved in helping all children learn. Teachers will be more challenged than ever. And, most importantly, our students will see immediate results.

The nation's public schools stand at an historic juncture. They are moribund institutions because they are organizations hopelessly out of sync with the realities of modern economic, social, and political life. They are a bureaucratic monopoly which cannot last. If schools stay as they are, they will be abandoned across the board, just as they have been in our great cities. Not long ago, our great cities were lighthouses, examples of best practice where the nation's best public schools thrived. No longer. The middle-class—black as well as white—has fled. Bright flight, not just white flight. It is not too much to assert that most of those left are those who have no choice.

The public at large has come to support choice in public schools. The nation's oldest and most complete tracking poll on public education appears each September in the *Phi Delta Kappan,* the most important magazine of the education profession. Performed by Gallup, and now in its twenty-fourth year, the *Annual Gallup Poll of the Public's Attitudes Toward the Public Schools* tells an extraordinary story. Asked if they would like to see vouchers adopted in this country, 50 percent agreed. This represents a major shift in public opinion, showing a climb between 1971—when 38 percent of respondents supported vouchers—to half the population twenty years later. Most surprising to most analysts is the breakdown of support; the most ardent supporters of vouchers (aside from private school parents, who support vouchers by 66 percent) are blacks and inner-city residents, 57 percent of whom support them. These findings are important in and of themselves, but they are most important in what they portend for public schools. When half of Americans support vouchers, the public schools must respond or face the public's wrath.

The public schools' response must be to extend the benefits of choice to the public sector. When they do, they will find overwhelming public support, much stronger than support for vouchers. Nationally, 62 percent of Americans support public school choice; indeed, only one significant category of respondents differs on the issue. Fifty percent of respondents over the age of fifty prefer public school choice, while 71 percent of those between eighteen and twenty-nine do. This powerful demographic difference cannot be ignored. Young people are more flexible and innovative than their elders. They are more willing to experiment. As well, many young families are used to choosing day-care arrangements, and find school choice equally natural. But perhaps most important, they are our most recent school graduates: They know whereof they speak.

In fairness, markets will not solve all problems. A part of the school restructuring task will be accomplished by creating a new curriculum; a part of the task will be accomplished by reconfiguring the use of time, from basic units of instruction to the length of the school day and school year; part of the task will be solved by technology, more inventive use of multimedia communications; and part of the problem will be solved by reorganizing and redeploying staff.

These things will not happen just because well-intentioned people want them to: only significant, intense, and continuing outside pressure will make them happen. That is the first and most important lesson of the market, and it is why public schools, to succeed, must submit to the "discipline" of the market. What is meant by such an assertion? Isn't the very idea of market discipline inconsistent with public schools? To the contrary, there are elements of the market that can be successfully adapted in the public sector, that will both revive and strengthen it.

One thing should be perfectly clear, however. Market discipline need not mean privatization, or private school choice, or direct aid to private schools. Those are legitimate and important subjects worthy of serious debate. But it is a separate debate. Public schools are our heritage, and with goodwill, hard work, and luck they will continue to be our future. It is no accident that the RJR Nabisco Foundation Next Century Schools program concentrated exclusively on *public* elementary, middle, and secondary schools. They are where the action is; they are where the problems exist. They enroll 88 percent of the nation's school-age children and spend $230 billion per year, and they enjoy a distinguished history, even though today's performance is inadequate. One sector should not be pitted against the other. The fact is, private schools are doing well. It is the public schools that are in deep trouble. Save them and the nation will prosper. Let them fail and we are all at risk. Left to the tender mercies of "reform by regulation," fail they will.

The Fundamentals of Supply and Demand

There are two broad dimensions to markets: supply and demand. How do public schools fit into this picture? The first question has to do with supply: Is it possible to think about market mechanisms without private ownership of the means of production? Can government-owned and -operated schools behave like private suppliers, demonstrating entrepreneurial qualities? The answer—which will be developed in the following pages—is a qualified yes. The demand side of markets—the role of the customer—raises the same question. Is it possible to think about markets without consumer sovereignty? The answer is no. For a market to function, the consumer must be "king." Not for a day, not for a week. Permanently. But this raises an interesting question of reciprocity. If the customer must be king, the supplier—the school and its staff—must, by definition, be in a position to respond to customer demand. Without the supplier's capacity to respond, the customer is trapped in a nonmarket; the consumer as "king" becomes consumer as "pretender." A stalemate.

And that is precisely what has happened to modern education in this country: stalemate. Teachers are trapped, students are trapped. Not because of ill-will or bad intentions, not because of scheming educators or servile politicians, but because schools are not organized to respond to the needs and interests of their students. They are bureaucratic monopolies that look like the factories of a vanished era; organized in a command and control hierarchy, they employ a demoralized workforce and rely upon a captive audience for customers. There are few incentives—and fewer rewards—to improve. Indeed, the "system" rewards caution and encourages playing it safe.

Look at one aspect of markets that has a bearing on schools. The classic definition of a functioning free market is one in which no single supplier or buyer can influence prices. Monopolies or providers who collude in restraint of trade can control price. But in free markets, neither buyer nor seller (acting alone) can set prices. In the case of public schools the issue is not so much price as collusion, which distorts normal market mechanisms. Multiple suppliers and consumers are important precisely because in numbers there is diversity, both as to supply and demand. It is through this mechanism that different tastes and interests are satisfied. Of course, public schooling will never be a perfect market, nor should it try to be. But public schools should use the best aspects of markets to strengthen and improve themselves, both in the short run and in the long run. An "economic" model of schooling—subject to the forces of supply and demand, diversity and autonomy, accountability and results—makes much more sense than the "political" model that we labor under today. In the "political" model, social and political processes conspire to force schools to a lowest common denominator. In the worst cases, actual corruption occurs, and schools become the site of patronage and worse. Our schools should be above politics. No one challenges citizen control over tax dollars and school policy; that is the right and proper thing. But elected school boards too frequently lose sight of their limited policymaking role and get intimately involved in the day-to-day operations of schools, "micromanaging" every aspect of the system. When this occurs it is no wonder that education becomes "politicized" and subject to compromises that end up satisfying almost no one.

The power of markets is precisely their capacity to minimize the need for unsatisfactory compromises. By bringing together willing buyers and sellers, markets harness voluntary interest and motivation. And as markets work in the humdrum world of consumer products, they are even more powerful in more complex and nuanced areas of life. Indeed, with the one exception of public elementary and secondary schools, markets are the rule in the learned professions: medicine, law, accounting, architecture, places of worship.

That is one of the principal reasons today's failing schools bear so little resemblance to institutions subject to market forces. The nation's most distressed schools are typically in the nation's most distressed neighborhoods, enrolling youngsters who have no other choice but to attend their local school. Yet the fault lies not in the customers—it is not the students' fault that they are attending second- or third-rate schools; given a choice they would select schools they liked just as they do their clothes and TV programs, with care and enthusiasm.

One thing the Next Century Schools program has revealed is that there is enormous talent and energy "out there" in the nation's schools just waiting to be released. Often the major barrier to excellence is "downtown." When "downtown" is supportive and flexible, schools have a higher chance of success. In addition to outstanding teachers and principals there is a common thread that runs through the most successful Next Century Schools: a superintendent and school board willing to "let go"; policymakers content to make policy and let the principal and teachers do what they're good at.

The Mooresville, North Carolina, Next Century School, Park View Elementary, was made possible by Sam Houston, a superintendent who believed in his teachers and principals. So too Raymond Poulin, Jr., in Guilford, Maine, who was willing to turn the principal and teachers of Piscataquis High School loose. Dr. Poulin says that he "gains power by giving it away." His authority is moral, not formal. These superintendents are like the nation's best CEO's; they "enable," they do not control and manipulate.

But these are small districts, where the problems are less acute to begin with. What of large districts? Charlotte-Mecklenburg, the nation's twenty-ninth biggest district, is a case in point. Superintendent John Murphy is determined to "make it work." That, he says, is the big challenge of the nineties; we now know how to make individual schools "work," but our huge districts are not working. The first step in Murphy's plan was to set district-wide performance standards; the second step is to enable building principals and teachers to reach those standards.

The tools will be radical decentralization, choice, magnet schools. The upside is success, the downside is failure, and schools that do not meet performance standards will be restructured. But how they meet those performance standards is up to them. It is no surprise that a pivotal school in Charlotte as it works through this process is a Next Century School, Highland-Tryon Hills, an elementary school serving an impoverished community that will rely on total quality management to transform itself.

TQM, or *total quality management,* is an idea forged on the anvil of business competition, but which has immediate and direct implications for public and not-for-profit organizations. It is a perfect example of the interplay of forces common to all large, complex organizations, whether or not they are profit-making. Any organization that uses TQM well is certain to improve. What is its secret? Hard work to be sure. More importantly, it is a way of looking at the world. In part the creation of Dr. William Edwards Deming, the father of statistical quality control, TQM has been brought to full bloom by the Xerox corporation. A genius without honor in his own land, Deming developed his approach during the Second World War. After the war he was virtually ignored in America, and went to Japan to assist in rebuilding the war-ravaged country. Deming was so successful that the Japanese named their highest civilian award, the Deming Prize, after him. Deming's principal insight is that errors in manufacturing and assembly, like errors in other enterprises, appear virtually at random; thus, the individual worker is not "responsible" for mistakes. It is the process—of which the worker is a part—that is responsible. Give workers the time and responsibility to manage their own work—as a "quality team," or as members of a "quality circle"—and errors virtually disappear. This image—so powerful to teachers—is a workplace without bosses. One in which workers are in charge, and one in which they are responsible. Given responsibility, they can be held accountable, without fear of adverse consequences.

Deming's insights have been taken to heart by numerous American corporations (and many schools in the last few years), but in no place more seriously than Xerox. As one of America's greatest success stories, Xerox found it difficult to find venture capital in the 1950s, then rose to unparalleled heights in the '60s, '70s, and early '80s, only to find itself in disastrous trouble in the mid and late '80s. Overtaken by vigorous and spirited competition, Xerox had gotten slack during its heyday. David Kearns pulled Xerox back from the brink, in large measure by using TQM. "Meet—exceed—customer requirements" became Xerox's rallying cry. So successful was Kearns's use of TQM that Xerox was one of the first U.S. companies to recover market share from the Japanese.

TQM, although created as a way to organize industrial activity, is well suited to schools. Reliance on autonomous work teams, which make decisions on their own about issues that affect team activity and output, is a "natural" for schools.

Next Century Schools, and other outstanding public schools and school districts, then, look like institutions subject to market discipline, and as a consequence, institutions that enjoy market rewards. This is nowhere more apparent than in the informal honor roll of American schools that educators, the public, and analysts know by name. In New York City, where public schools of choice have been the norm for generations, there is a long list of distinguished public schools: Brooklyn Tech, Hunter College grade school and high school, Aviation, The Bronx High School of Science, Stuyvesant, Murry Bergtraum, LaGuardia School of the Performing Arts. This list of older schools is joined by Central Park East (one of the network of Ted Sizer's Essential Schools), the middle schools of Spanish Harlem's District 4, and the old Benjamin Franklin High School on FDR Drive at 116th, restructured and renamed the Manhattan School of Science and Mathematics. Once the school with the highest drop-out rate in New York City, the Manhattan School of Science and Mathematics—a K-12 school "adopted" by the GE Foundation—sends *all* of its graduates on to college. And it graduates the whole class: no drop-outs.

Magnet Schools

Magnet schools or other "choice" schools—designed to "attract" students (and teachers) by the power of their curriculum and organization—are not just the elite math-science institutions. Career, vocational, and technical schools are critically important as well. According to the *New York Times,* Columbia University's Teachers College "praises New York City as a national model for its career magnet schools, which draw students from across the city and prepare them both for specific careers and college." The study's lead author, sociologist Robert Crain, describes New York's magnets as "the most exciting set of choices for a student in high school. All the chronic problems big cities have are as bad here as anywhere else, but at the same time there are these experimental schools. It's like a swamp—there are these mangrove trees growing out of it that are quite amazing." The list goes on: Boston Latin, Philadelphia Boys and Philadelphia Girls High Schools, Lowell in San Francisco, the North Carolina School of Science and Mathematics (a Next Century School). Each of these is an autonomous public school that draws on a region for its student body, not just a neighborhood, and is selected by students—and frequently selects students—in much the way a regional college or university does.

But the nation's list of superb schools is not restricted to magnet schools. Nor do most of the communities that are home to distinguished research facilities, colleges, or universities, contain magnet schools. Yet almost without exception, each of these communities boasts a first-rate "neighborhood" school: Oak Ridge, Tennessee; Los Alamos, New Mexico; Ann Arbor, Michigan; Princeton, New Jersey; Chapel Hill, North Carolina; and Minneapolis, Minnesota, are examples.

Almost without exception these schools look like neighborhood schools, a part of the "bureaucratic monopoly" we disdain. But appearances can be deceiving. These schools are "selected" in a powerfully important way by the nation's most discriminating consumers, the parents who work and live in those communities. They have been deliberately chosen because of their reputations for high quality, for meeting—indeed, exceeding—"customer requirements." Schools of this kind act as though they are part of a market because they are; their product happens to be "upscale," high-powered education, and their competition is not so much other public schools, but demanding, prestigious private schools.

The school boards, superintendents, principals, and teachers in these communities know that they are being held to high standards, and they must meet them or face an irate public and declining enrollment as parents turn instead to private schools. A set of reciprocal expectations characterizes these schools as well—parents expect the schools to deliver and the schools expect the parents to perform.

Even the most ardent supporter of markets may be skeptical about the extent to which they will make a difference with schools. Except as a metaphor and stimulus to change, what do markets really have to do with public schools? Are there real lessons and real practices that can be drawn from experience with markets that have a direct bearing on public schools? There are. But first, the most important generalization about markets: Their essence is *the voluntary coming together of suppliers and customers.* Why is this important?

Voluntary association harnesses motivation, the key to success in any enterprise, public or private. Too often people think of markets only in terms of profits and competition.

32

True, these factors are important, because they are central to markets, but there is a motive force in markets, a justification for their existence. A market is simply the most effective system known for creating and distributing wealth. Whatever its imperfections, it is better than the alternatives.

Markets are first and foremost a communication system: They provide information on availability, quality, quantity, variety, and finally, price. Markets let buyers know what is available and sellers know what is wanted—in what quantity, at what quality, at what price.

Communication is important because it brings together willing buyers and willing sellers. Which raises the question of price. How much is the buyer willing to pay, how much does the seller demand? For the noneconomist, here is the most startling and most important aspect of markets: Cost does not determine price. This is an idea so unlikely—so "counterintuitive"—that it bears repeating: *Cost does not determine price.* What does determine price, and what difference does it make? Price is determined by what a willing buyer and a willing seller agree to. Producers must sell above cost to stay in business. This simple fact is the heart of markets. Only monopolies can set prices. And that is why they gouge consumers, whether they are private monopolies or public monopolies of the kind that used to characterize the former Soviet Union. Alone among economic systems, markets provide powerful—indeed, irresistible—incentives for producers to create more efficient utilization of resources. Markets reduce unit cost and increase output. Profit is the producers' reward for doing so. This is the core of how markets reward success and penalize failure.

And the key player in markets is the entrepreneur. Who is the entrepreneur? The person who reconfigures uses of capital and labor. The entrepreneur may be a risk-taker—indeed, frequently is a risk-taker—but the entrepreneur does not take risks for their own sake. As internationally renowned management guru Peter Drucker points out, the entrepreneur seizes opportunity. Typically, the biggest "risk" the entrepreneur takes is to swim against the tide of the conventional wisdom. "We've always done it this way," is the cry of the bureaucrat. The entrepreneur does it differently and more effectively.

Creating educational entrepreneurs is the overriding objective of Next Century Schools; educational venture capital is the tool; the result is new, different, and more effective schools. Only if market forces are permitted to operate in public schools, can the lessons of Next Century Schools be broadly diffused.

The effect of reconfiguring the mix of capital and labor is that the entrepreneur lowers the price for the same quality or holds price constant and increases quality. But most important, the entrepreneur will go beyond new ways to do old things—old wine in new bottles; the true entrepreneur will design and bring to market things people do not yet know they want or need—serious things like air bags or the Xerox machine, enjoyable things like Lifesavers holes or mini-Oreos, frivolous things like bikinis. In each case the "customer" did not know he or she needed or wanted the product—or service—until it became available.

The entrepreneur—the superintendent, principal, or teacher—then, must work in an environment in which risk is not frowned upon and in which success will be rewarded. In the world of education the pattern is the same, whether it was the introduction of the first mass-produced textbooks—which made mass education possible—or the use of interactive computer video, which will transform the way in which people learn as well as the speed with which they learn.

Technology

But note the slow pace of adoption of technology in education; the whole enterprise remains much as it was in the time of the ancient Greeks. The reason is not that there are no technologies that would make a difference in schools—there are many that would. The reason is not just that technology is costly—though educators think it is. There are technologies available for schools that would pay for themselves just as they do in the private sector. The reason is that because schools are regulated bureaucracies, they are not organized in ways that lead them to the introduction of technology. They are like eighteenth-century farms, not even ready to dream about the agricultural revolution that would sweep the world in the nineteenth and twentieth centuries.

The introduction and use of technology is not unique to market economies—the wheel, the lever, and the Archimedean screw predate capitalism by many centuries. Yet of all economic systems, market economies are the most favorably disposed toward technology. Why? Because of the signals they send and the environment they create. Markets encourage people to think about increased efficiencies and economies, and to utilize them even if they mean a complete change in the way business is transacted. And typically, introducing a new technology is disorienting and dislocating. Only the fact that it will increase performance justifies it. That is why technologies diffuse only slowly in traditional societies and within traditional institutions.

In the modern, high-tech West, schools offer a powerful insight into this phenomenon. Rarely do educators think about technology because they are insulated from market forces. When educators need to "increase" outputs—higher test scores, for example—they ask for increased "inputs"— more money and staff. When margins shrink in the private sector, managers look for ways to increase efficiency; when margins shrink in the public sector, public sector managers look for additional resources to offset inefficiencies.

The most striking evidence of this process at work is the educators' lament about technology: "We can't afford it." Who has not heard it? How does the private sector differ in this regard? Just the opposite claim is advanced on behalf of important technologies: "We can't afford not to." These different views speak volumes about the nature of the process. Effective and useful technologies are self-liquidating, they pay for themselves—over time—and then return a "profit," excess income that may be further invested to produce future profits.

Technology is easy to talk about, but hard to visualize without examples. Let us supply a few for illustrative purposes. The Conference Board estimates that 60 percent of all Americans now use a keyboard at some point during their work week and that number will increase over time. How has typing—or "keyboarding" as it is now called—been taught traditionally? By a teacher in a classroom of twenty to thirty students, each hunched over an Underwood Upright (one of the great old typing warhorses of the twentieth century), who "study" and practice typing for fifty minutes a day for a semester or two. They are then given a grade—A, B, C, D. This is typing at its most low-tech.

What is high-tech typing? No teacher, no fixed time periods, no grades—just a computer and a self-guided typing software program. The best known is probably *Mavis Beacon's Typing Tutor.* While there are many programs on the market, they all share one trait: the student does the work because it is fun, interesting, and challenging. One popular program uses "letter invaders"—a typing lesson modeled on arcade games. In this case, enemy invaders are "shot down" by the student's use of the correct keys. Teachers and time-limited teaching are not only unnecessary, but undesirable. With high-tech typing, students work on keyboard skills as they need them. Finally, grades are irrelevant. Students learn to type at a level of proficiency consistent with their occupational or professional goals. For instance, a newspaper reporter who can type 45 words a minute with 80 percent accuracy is good enough (so long as his computer contains a spell checker); a court reporter, even with a spell checker on the computer, will need to type 90 words a minutes with 100 percent accuracy.

What's true of typing is true of the whole curriculum. For example, the U.S. Naval Academy has developed an interactive computer video disk program for language instruction that will soon be available to the nation as a whole. Using real-time satellite downloading of foreign language TV programs, the Naval Academy language faculty loads portions of the programs onto a laser disk. The faculty then builds in lessons—queries, questions, interrogatories—as well as assignments; the students are virtually on their own. The system uses full-color monitors, stereophonic sound, full-motion graphics, stills, text, and complete interactivity. It is a far cry from the primitive tape-recorder language labs which evoke painful memories among most former students.

The final results are not yet in, but it is clear that Naval officers in training are learning more, faster, and at a lower unit cost than ever before. Has the Naval Academy used this as an opportunity to release language teachers and save money? To the relief of the teachers and students, they have not. But students are expected to learn more—to become proficient, not merely parroting language. The issue is an important one in a global economy in which America has global military responsibilities; most Naval officers can expect a language-specific assignment during their career, and knowledge of a foreign language is a powerful asset, both to the individual officers and to the service as a whole.

In this way, markets create incentives to save and invest, an idea foreign to most of the public sector. Typically, public-sector spending is treated as operating expenses, not "investment." In part this simply reflects long-standing practices and habits; public-sector "investments" are usually thought of in terms of bricks and mortar. This is so because most public spending is from current revenues for current costs. Yet the lesson of the late twentieth century is that there is no investment more important than "investing in our children," the title of the Committee for Economic Development policy statement on education released in 1985. As the title implies, we can no longer afford the luxury of treating education as an expense; it is an investment. In the future. In the students and in society as a whole.

For whom do markets exist, then? They exist for the benefit of consumers; the fact that they function by rewarding efficient and responsive producers with income is simply to the consumer's ultimate advantage. Efficient producers benefit consumers. Efficient schools benefit students and society at large. And consumers penalize inefficient and unresponsive producers by withholding income.

There is, of course, more to markets than price competition between goods and services. When a good—or service—becomes "too expensive," particularly if demand for it is inelastic, substitution occurs, and less costly products enter the market—plastic for metal, for example. But there is an equally interesting aspect of markets that has a special bearing on education: the creation of market niches, where specialty production occurs, in which goods—and now more frequently services—are tailored to special needs, demands, and interests.

One of the reasons technology is weakly developed in the nation's elementary and secondary schools is that normal market processes that lead to technological innovation in the rest of the economy don't exist in schools. School budgets, for example, rarely permit substituting one category of expenditure for another; thus, a school that might prefer twenty computers to an additional teacher aide is not able to make that change. This inflexibility is not limited to public schools, by any means. Private, for-profit concerns can be inflexible if competitive pressure is not brought to bear. British newspapers were wedded to obsolete technology and refused to change until the *International Wall Street Journal* began to appear on London streets hours before the British dailies—with obvious implications for readership. Fleet Street quickly changed.

If the demand is great enough, the niche will be occupied by other providers, but if it is a small niche, a "naturally occurring" monopoly will appear. It may be due to geographic isolation—in which the nature of the terrain permits only a single producer to appear—or it may be due to highly specialized tastes and interests. For example, for many years Montessori education attracted a small but devoted following, and one school would serve a large geographic area. Only as the approach became more widely known and more popular did the number of providers increase.

One central aspect of markets is "marketing," or communicating about what is available—on both the supply side and the demand side—and developing those products, goods, and services for which there is a demand or *for which demand can be created.* Some Americans are critical of the idea of stimulating demand, as though it is simply a process of separating gullible customers from their money. No doubt this has been true in some cases, but by "stimulating demand," invaluable products which no one knew they would ever need have been invented: things such as the Xerox 914, the IBM PC, facsimile transmission, the microwave oven, Federal Express, the cellular phone, and ATM banking. These are all examples of products and services that are highly regarded and almost universally available today, yet no one—except the visionary designers—knew anyone "needed" any one of these before they existed. Now we can't do without them. What does this have to do with schools? A good deal. Look at Park View Elementary in Mooresville, North Carolina.

Determined to introduce year-round schooling, even though many community members were skeptical and even hostile, school officials had a major marketing challenge on their hands. Convinced that year-round schooling meant better education at a lower cost, the educators had to sell the idea to the community. They did, but it took time, hard work, and energy. As Mooresville Superintendent Sam Houston points out, the most vigorous opponents of year-round schooling were the first to sign up. Why? In the first instance they were the most actively involved and well-informed parents, yet they saw no need to change. When Sam and his principals and teachers convinced these parents, they had all the fervor of converts. If it sounds like the Xerox 914 story, it should; no one knew they needed or wanted plain paper copies until they were a reality. It took Chester Carlson, inventor of xerography, to understand that.

Cooperation and Collaboration

It is in this connection that the least noted but most important aspect of markets surfaces: cooperation and collaboration. Not to be confused with conspiracy in restraint of trade, genuine cooperation, both within the firm and between firms, lies at the heart of markets. Modern production techniques—in particular in the service sector—represent triumphs of cooperation and collaboration, as people work toward shared goals. Indeed, that is precisely what the modern firm is all about. And cooperation among firms as they participate in functioning markets is essential, both to permit communication among the players and to provide for orderly transitions.

Finally, there is the narrow segment of the competitive market with which schools are analogous: high-tech, high-performance companies and human-capital-intensive associations, corporations and partnerships: law firms, joint medical practices, architectural and accounting firms, and yes, churches and synagogues (which in many respects are the most apt institutional comparison for schools). These institutions compete with each other in a very special way; they reveal, produce, or sell highly specialized knowledge—solutions to problems—reflecting their own talents and interests and the talents and interests of their clients, patrons, or parishoners. Their most distinctive characteristic is discrete market segmentation—an anesthesiologist rarely operates, just as a surgeon rarely administers anesthesia; so too, architects, accountants, and lawyers specialize, and will recommend competing firms to clients whose needs they cannot fill themselves.

Putting schools in a market setting is not without foundation. A private school market exists, and it is instructive. It has three salient characteristics. Private schools are sharply focused; they know what they are doing. Private schools are small. While there are more than 20,000 private schools in the nation, only a tiny handful have enrollments that exceed 1,000 students, and those are typically separated on more than one campus. And private school "systems" are weak to nonexistent. Indeed, only Catholic, diocesan schools are members of anything that resembles a "system," and even that is attenuated. In Chicago, for example, where a half million youngsters attend public school, there are 3,500 public school administrators. Compare the Catholic schools: Almost half the number of students are overseen by thirty-five administrators. Private schools are not parts of "chains" or systems for a reason; they are convinced that autonomy and institutional independence is a virtue, to be treasured.

And what of private school focus? To use Peter Drucker's powerful distinction, they are interested in optimizing, not maximizing. That is why private schools are universally smaller than their public counterparts. Not only are there almost no economies of scale in education, most teachers and principals agree that optimal school size is smaller rather than larger. The competitive pressures, then, combine to encourage schools to be small, not large, and autonomous, not part of a "chain."

Markets are voluntary—not only customers are volunteers, though. Producers voluntarily decide what to produce, how much to produce, and on what terms. Market entry, then, is a critical variable in terms of success; ease of entry means a large, highly motivated pool of providers. Think of an environment in which teachers and principals could start and run their own schools. Many observers—educators in particular—focus on the downside of markets. And there are problems to be sure. Markets fail, or slip toward failure. People with limited resources cannot acquire costly goods or services; health care is a case in point. Queues form, and those at the end of the queue are often precisely those who need to be at the head, because their problems are acute.

Incomplete information makes it difficult for people to participate in markets fully and effectively, and occasionally outright fraud and deceit occur. But these are problems of human nature as much as problems of markets. As in any fallible venture, markets should not be measured by their excesses but by their successes. No form of human organization has produced more wealth and distributed it more widely than market economies.

Perhaps most important, in the West we learned long ago that government can intervene in the event of market failure, real or impending. Markets are not perfect; creative intervention can smooth the rough spots. Insurance can distribute risk more equitably, public information sources can increase knowledge about product quality and availability, thoughtful regulation can smooth transitions and protect the unwary, income protection and redistribution can restore balance.

So far we have talked about choosing schools in general terms. What are the underlying reasons for letting parents choose, however? The answer is deceptively simple: no one—certainly no remote bureaucrat—has a better sense of the child's interests than the parent. This is not to suggest that parents are all experts on child development, curriculum, or pedagogy; obviously, few are. But the issue is not

43

what they know so much as why they care. They care for the same reasons parents everywhere have always cared. What they need is information, the capacity to make reasoned and well-informed decisions about their children. This capacity, of course, is the essence of markets—that's what they are all about. And that's where teachers and principals come in.

Who knows better a teacher's capacities, talents, interests—and limitations—than the teacher himself or herself? And what better way to harness energy and enthusiasm than to bring teachers into the schools they like and want to work in? It is through this conjunction of supply and demand that teachers become true professionals; they make their services available to interested clients in a market. In so doing they run real risks—there may be no takers for their services. But the prospect of success is even higher. For once they find "customers," the professionals know how to tailor their activities to these customers' needs.

Markets do not leave participants at the mercy of each other—that is the special province of monopolies. Markets reinforce expertise, particularly in the learned professions, and education is no exception. Teachers and principals are "selling" what they know and are able to do. And that is precisely what parents and students are "buying." They are in the market for competence.

In some respects, Next Century Schools look like sole proprietorships—or as cynics might note, cottage industries—because they stand alone. True, each Next Century School is part of a school system, but in most cases the rest of the system has watched and waited, not imitated. That is next, because when the Next Century School models are more widely diffused, they will become the new norm. The Highland-Tryon Hills Elementary School, one of the poorest and most racially isolated in Charlotte, North Carolina, is one of 113 schools in the nation's twenty-ninth largest school district. In Charlotte, choice is becoming the norm, as the district implements board policy to increase the range of school choice across the district, and Highland-Tryon parents and teachers will find choice as "natural" in the future as they find neighborhood assignment today. Charlotte-Mecklenburg school district was the first large district in the nation to fall under court order to integrate. Twenty-five years later the *Swann* decision has been lifted because Charlotte has successfully integrated. With minimal white flight, harmonious race relations, a sophisticated school board, and a savvy superintendent, John Murphy, it was possible for Charlotte to move beyond *Swann*.

What are the new terms that made it possible for the court to lift *Swann*? Schools of choice. Magnet schools. Schools with distinctive academic and pedagogical personalities. Schools that teachers want to teach in, that parents want to participate in, and that students want to attend. Indeed, public school choice—usually magnet schools—has become the preferred vehicle for the U.S. courts to accelerate racial integration. Schools that are poor and racially isolated, however, have been permitted to remain single-race schools because they are *Milikanized* (a term of art that emerged from a court case in Michigan under then Governor Milikan: Courts permit single-race minority schools to remain in place if there is no feasible alternative *and* substantial extra resources are made available for them). Soon, however, Highland's students will be able to compete with the best Charlotte has to offer, and they too will begin to participate in the district-wide choice plan. That is Superintendent Murphy's long-term objective: 113 magnet schools!

Accountability

And that is why the question of educational account-ability—a conundrum in a monopoly setting—is answered so powerfully in a market setting. As John Coons and Steven Sugarman eloquently point out in their book *Education by Choice,* the ends of education are "indeterminate." By this they mean there is no master template that can be applied to education, no one "best system," no one "best school," no best way to measure "output," particularly in the context of a regulated monopoly. If schools were like prison license-plate factories, production norms and targets could be set and measured, and precise judgments about the relative efficiency of one prison license-plate factory as compared to another could be reached.

But what schools do—and how they do it—cannot be compared to a production process; ultimate accountability for schools must be customer satisfaction: students, parents, employers, and taxpayers in general. Just as schools cannot be "regulated" into becoming better institutions, accountability will ultimately be achieved not by using quantitative measures alone but by meeting a market test: satisfying customers. Permitting families to choose schools is the ultimate form of accountability, because with it, the would-be monopolist cannot take customers for granted.

The logic and inescapable corollary of selecting schools is school diversity and specialization; since there is not one way to design and operate schools, an education market will produce as much diversity and variety as the minds of suppliers can conceive and buyers can demand. Already in the private sector the range of offerings is wide and varied, running from Montessori schools to military academies, from fundamentalist religious schools to secular day schools, from boarding schools to Waldorf schools (where youngsters learn to read after they have cut their permanent teeth). This cornucopia exists because different teachers, parents, and students have very different ideas about what works and why. The truth is deceptively simple: Different things work for different people—some of us require more structure than others, some more free time; some flourish with old-fashioned phonics, some do better with a whole-language approach; some schools believe that computer labs are more useful than computers in each classroom.

These differences are not a matter of caprice or simple idiosyncrasy; rather, as Next Century Schools reveal, they are the product of genuinely different views of education, and the willingness to be guided by the needs and demands of customers. At Bloomfield Hills, students and parents want a school that will send most students on to college with superior skills and creative imaginations. At Linda Vista Elementary School the need is for native-language instruction for children from many countries. At Davis Elementary, the focus is on mathematics. In each case the specialization is operating within a framework of accountability: providing what is needed and wanted in a particular community.

Meeting Customer Requirements

The result of an education market is responsiveness on the part of providers—they meet customer requirements. But responsiveness is a two-way street. Patrons are more responsive as well. Concerned about school quality in the first instance—after all, they have gone to the trouble to find the school and enroll in it—patrons are prepared to meet the de-

mands the school places on them: homework, parent participation, support for extracurriculars, volunteering and men-
toring, painting and fixing up if necessary. The school that is
chosen—by staff and families—is a school that is both flexible and responsive.

"Choosing" a school does not necessarily come naturally,
at least in the beginning. Mooresville, North Carolina's Next
Century School, Park View Elementary, had to be "sold" to
the community. Marketing year-round schools turned out to
be one of the biggest tasks before the teachers and principal
because of substantial community reluctance to change tried-
and-true ways of doing things. Now three years into the program, Mooresville has more takers than space. The program
has been an overwhelming success, and it turns out that the
community members most skeptical about the benefits of
year-round schools in the beginning are now among the
most ardent supporters.

Critics of market mechanisms in the schools are quick to
note that their advantages are "middle-class" advantages,
that the poor and disadvantaged will have difficulty taking
advantage of them. Less likely to be well informed, the poor
will not enjoy the benefits of responsive schools because
they will not know to enroll in them to begin with. There are
two answers to this important charge: first, markets work to
everyone's advantage, not just those consumers who are
most active in seeking out value. There is a significant spill-
over in markets, and consumers who are somewhat less diligent than the wisest shoppers enjoy the benefits of their
more aggressive colleagues. A store sensitive to the demands of the most discriminating patron serves all patrons
equally well. Second, the poor and dispossessed, no less
than their more fortunate neighbors, should have a moral
right to choose, and to operate in an environment where

they are treated like competent human beings. Though they may in the first instance make mistakes because they have little experience in choosing, they should not be denied for that reason. To the contrary, they will only learn to choose wisely and well by choosing.

Markets are the best analogy for schools even if they are not perfect; where they are not perfect, the authorities can and must intervene to correct inequities. How, for example, should school boards deal with questions of racial isolation using a market analogy? The answer has been provided by experience across the country: "controlled choice." Today, "controlled choice" is the preferred tool of the federal courts to achieve racial integration and maintain racial balance. The formulation is straightforward; any child in the system is permitted to move—to select the school he or she wishes to attend—so long as that move improves racial balance. With a stroke, "white flight" is eliminated—without busing. In Charlotte-Mecklenburg, for example, a district that has been under court order to bus for two decades, magnet schools are being created across the district to both eliminate busing and achieve and assure lasting racial balance. Why do magnet schools work where busing has failed? Because markets work voluntarily. No compulsion. People chose to be together. And it works!

For magnet schools to work effectively, school boards must insist on truth-in-advertising; schools should be expected to present truthful information about themselves to prospective patrons. Perhaps most important, school boards should be expected to support informational outreach programs to keep their citizens informed about what schools are doing and what they propose to do.

There is a final dimension to meeting customer requirements that is the special province of professionals (as distinct from businesses which sell goods and services). In many cases, customers don't know what their "requirements" are, except in the broadest sense. Medicine, architecture, law, education, and religion are all cases in point. The client, patient, parishioner, or student establishes a relationship with only a dim sense of what he or she needs or wants. They know they want health or good design or spiritual succor, but it is up to the professional to provide it. It is not just that adults know more than children—though they do—but that professionals know more than their clients. The same principle applies to teachers and principals. The question arises, however: How do you enlist someone for an activity that will be good for them but which they do not know they need? Teachers, forever and everywhere, have been plagued by this dilemma. Grades, tracking, holding kids back have all been tried, with limited success. It has fallen to Mooresville to finesse the problem in a larger and more sophisticated setting. Year-round schools in Mooresville, North Carolina, are voluntary. The 180 days of regular schooling is required by North Carolina statute, but "intersessions," or three-week intervals between the sixty-day trimesters, are voluntary; they are available for remediation, day care, or enrichment. In this case, the teachers determine who needs what. They meet customer requirements by assigning children to the proper class.

School Boards

School boards are the linchpin of school governance, and their role must change if market forces are to make a difference to public schools in the future. Too often school boards succumb to the temptation to "micromanage." It is easy to understand why. Buffeted by the most intense and emotional issues before us as a society, school boards are expected to exercise Solomonic judgment on every issue imaginable, from drugs and AIDS education to teen pregnancy, juvenile delinquency, the impact of broken homes, and the devastating effects of poverty. Often serving without pay, school board members work for long hours at what must seem to many to be thankless tasks.

No one said their jobs would be easy, and easy they are not. But a large part of the difficulty school boards confront is the fact that they are expected to oversee a system that is not "self-regulating"—as markets are—but a system that requires constant regulation. It does so for two major reasons. First, in the modern era schools have been managed almost exclusively in terms of "inputs": the number of kids in the building, the number of buildings in the system, the number of principals and staff, the number of books in the library, the number of meals served a day, the number of buses and bus drivers, the number of crossing guards. The input most talked about, of course, is money.

Inputs are important, make no mistake. But they are only important in terms of their impact on "outputs." Outputs are what markets are about. Outputs are what schooling is about. Outputs—the difference going to school makes. If outputs become the focus of concern, the role of inputs is better understood and explained. In particular the "cost" of different inputs, and the cost of configuring inputs differently to achieve different outputs, becomes an issue about which people may exchange reasonable ideas. As things stand today, however, everything that schools do is explained in terms of inputs, and any change or improvement can only be understood by increasing inputs. Thus, if enrollments increase, schools need more money; if enrollments decrease, schools need more money. If test scores go down, schools need more money; if they go up, they need more money. The fact is that input measurement is inevitably a one-way street; if inputs are the metric, the only way—by definition—to improve is to increase inputs. There is no limit. By way of illustration, for well over a century American schools have systematically reduced class size, even though there is no research to support the idea that smaller classes produce higher outcomes. University of Michigan professor Eric Hanushek's "meta-analysis" of over 150 class-size studies show no improvement in student outcomes as class size is reduced. Yet the pressure to reduce class size continues, because that is one of the few things schools count. If, by way of contrast, schools measured outcomes more carefully, and reported that test scores of students go up dramatically when students are tutored by older youngsters (as they do), a very different conclusion would emerge. Output measurement will make two things possible: a better understanding of inputs, and the end of detailed regulation. School boards can provide overall guidance for objectives— outputs—and let schools, teachers, and principals, reach those objectives as they think best.

Second, school boards have been led to believe that all the schools under their control should be as nearly identical as possible, as though education was a perfectly uniform process. Next Century Schools show clearly that cookie-cutter schools are the problem, not the solution. But the attempt to make all schools alike is never-ending; indeed, it reinforces all the worst aspects of management-by-regulation. Regulations, typically crafted to limit or eliminate worse-case behavior, of necessity sink to the lowest common denominator. Regulations designed to prevent egregious behavior have the effect of inhibiting excellent behavior as well. Regulations become a floor and a ceiling, through which the worst are not supposed to fall, but through which the best cannot rise.

Indeed, the only way for the gifted teacher or principal to escape from the clutches of regulation is to become a "canny outlaw," a rule-bender and avoider. One of the best examples of this is the set of reforms that came to pass in Spanish Harlem when Sy Fliegel was Assistant Superintendent. Asked how he could get away with sweeping reform, he casually observed that he never asked for permission and never told the bureaucrats at 110 Livingston Street (the New York City HQ) what was going on.

What did Fliegel do? With the support of his district superintendent, Anthony Alvarado, he created an elementary school "choice" system in Spanish Harlem, one of the most poverty-stricken places in the United States. Today, children in District 4 are able to choose which public school they will attend, based solely on its academic offerings. The system is so popular that youngsters from other parts of New York City enroll in District 4—true testimony to its success. Why did Fliegel do it? His answer is to the point: "I believe that what's good enough for rich kids is good enough for poor kids."

The metaphor of the market offers school boards two solutions—one modest, one ambitious—to what is truly the tar-baby dilemma: Once you start micromanaging it's almost impossible to stop. The modest solution is to design a program of management by exception, and let those schools that are truly good do their own thing. Deregulate them, across the board. Then the school board can devote its attention to matters of policy, and insofar as it feels the need to keep its eye on individual schools, it can attend to those that are in academic or other trouble. The other solution—one that is both long term and more powerful—is to step back from regulation altogether and begin to frame output and performance measures for schools. By this device the board retains control of essential elements, avoids micromanagement, and lays the groundwork for programs that will reward success and provide incentives for improvement.

One of the main problems, one endemic to public education, is the need to fashion a smoothly functioning means of market entry; in the private sector as well as the public, existing providers prefer to see market entry limited. And not for altruistic reasons. The fewer the players, the richer the pickings, particularly for products and services for which demand is largely inelastic.

Public schools are no exception to this general rule; indeed, not only do they resist new players in the field, as the nation's population has spiraled upward, the number of school districts has plummeted, from 130 thousand districts before World War II, when the population was less than 150 million people, to 15,700 districts today, with a population of 250 million. Most amazing, while the number of high school students has tripled and the graduation rate has doubled, the number of high schools has been nearly static.

What is clearly needed in today's climate is significantly eased terms of market entry, in which new public schools could appear so long as they meet minimum criteria. The logical "founders" of such institutions would be existing public school teachers and principals, eager to gain intellectual and administrative independence. The idea, though novel, is hardly farfetched; New York City's magnet schools are schools of this kind, and Detroit, Michigan, school board president Larry Patrick's efforts to create "Charter Schools" are another. The purpose and function of such schools is to be a part of the public system without being subject to burdensome and counterproductive bureaucracy.

Not surprisingly, the question of cost is raised in connection with magnet schools, charter schools, and other "special" schools. Don't they all cost more, and if so, isn't that the secret of their success? "Give us more money and we could do it too," is the frequently heard complaint. The answer has two tiers. On the one hand, in the established examination schools in New York City (Stuyvesant, Brooklyn Tech, or Bronx High School of Science) for example, the costs are the same as the average city allocation for high schools because the district will not spend any more. On the other hand, in one atypical Next Century School, the North Carolina School of Science and Mathematics, per pupil expenditures appear to be much higher than the state average. It is, after all, a boarding school, with small class sizes and elaborate laboratories; one expects higher costs than other schools. But the question remains: Does it really cost more? The answer: More than what? The fact is, as a nation we use the wrong metric to measure education costs. We compare per pupil costs based on input. How many kids attend school how long, is the question that is usually asked. But it's the wrong question. The real question is, What does it cost to learn a given amount of material? What does mastery cost? There are two answers. First, no matter what it costs it's usually cheaper than the alternative: ignorance. It's no surprise that 70 percent of convicts are school drop-outs. Second, mastery in a good school is usually a bargain compared to the cost of second-rate schools. School cost is typically cast in terms of dollars per student over time. Thus, a four-year high school that produces 400 graduates per year at a cost of $4,000 per student per year will have spent $16,000 per graduate (400 × $4,000), or $1,600,000 per graduating class (400

× $4,000). Neither number is very useful in terms of education output; much more useful is knowing how much a student learns. Imagine two high schools that spend the same, but in one school students learn twice as much as the other (for example, in one school all the students earn at least a score of three on several advanced placement examinations; in the other school no one scores above one). In this example, the cost of learning—or the return on investment—is much more favorable in one school than the other.

In some ways the most promising element of market discipline for public schools is cost control. The true power of markets is to bring down costs of production and delivery of goods and services, by encouraging and rewarding efficiency. Not expenditures, but cost. Unit cost. Indeed, in the industrialized democracies, productivity increases—greater efficiencies in production—have been the source of both increased national wealth and increased personal wealth. Productivity increases mean the economic pie actually gets bigger; for a given input, there is more output. Not just more profits for owners, but more income for workers as well.

As things stand today, public schools offer no metric—no way to measure results—that permits us to say we are spending too much, too little, or just the right amount. Markets, while not perfect, can help move us toward an answer to that question. Schools in a market setting will be strongly encouraged to optimize—to do what they are good at, to learn to do it better, and to set goals that are both high and realistic. The reason? They will be rewarded for it. Not with more students—though some schools will choose to grow larger if demand for their services is strong—but by a much clearer sense of accountability. And a greater sense of efficacy.

Diverse schools, each with a distinctive academic and

pedagogical personality, will have the opportunity and responsibility to serve their student body as efficiently as possible. Parents and students will expect it; teachers and principals will soon find it second nature. Schools will for the first time think before they routinely fill a teaching vacancy; might that same amount of money be more effectively spent for teacher aides or computers or some mix of both?

Indeed, technology, which is today treated by most schools as an attractive and entertaining add-on (or a "subject" to be studied rather than as a tool to be used), will, in a market regime, have the opportunity to become an integral part of instruction. Might each teacher in the building have a telephone? They alone among professionals are "phoneless," an astonishing fact when you consider that teachers talk for a living, and could benefit from having homework hotlines and computer modems to better allow them to help their students.

At a more complex level, might there be serious tradeoffs between people and technology? Are typing teachers needed, when there are computer programs like *Mavis Beacon's Typing Tutor*? This program—and others like it—is not only self-guided, it sets and keeps a pace suited to the student, and it replaces, in one fell swoop, the idea that a course called typing should meet so many hours for so many weeks and be overseen by an adult called a teacher.

In the new school, typing should be "learned" by students, working together on computers, and not taught by anyone. A student mentor, fulfilling a community service requirement, could provide the guidance and support novice typists might need, and pave the way to genuine computer literacy. Indeed, does anyone doubt that kids know more about computers than adults? Is there an adult anywhere who can program a VCR without the help of a kid? So too, the whole curriculum. In the school of the future, the teacher will be too important to stand around and "teach"; rather, he or she will manage instruction as students learn in a variety of ways with a variety of formats.

The most important aspect of markets is what the great Viennese economist Joseph Schumpeter called "creative destruction." Alone among forms of social and economic organization, free markets—capitalism—provide for the disappearance (or fundamental reorganization) of weak and failing institutions. Businesses that do not pass the market test of satisfying their customers, fold; so do not-for-profits that rely on patronage to keep going. Schools that do not meet customer requirements should also close. The only institution that can survive market failure without restructuring or collapsing is the monopoly, whether it is the "private" monopoly of the West, protected by the state through law and regulation, or the "public" monopoly that brought ruin to the Soviet Union. In a market, what happens when providers become noncompetitive? They change their ways or go out of business—unless they have access to the police power of the state. Then they form monopolies, or institute tariffs, or restrict trade, to insulate themselves from competitive pressures.

This chapter closes with an ironic observation: America needs greater choice among public schools because the "choices" now available produce perverse results. Today, parents with the money for a down payment in an exclusive suburb (or city neighborhood) and the insight and enthusiasm necessary to find better schools, do find better schools. They buy their way in. They actively choose to enroll their children in good schools. And if they cannot find a public school that suits them, they will find a private school that does. This system works passably well for parents with the means and the energy to seek out schools that serve their needs and interests, but poorly for the dispossessed and the poor.

No one's social interests are served by a system that concentrates the poor in one set of schools, the well-to-do in another. It is not only undemocratic, it creates a poor economic environment. Put most simply, the poor—those who need good schools the most—are least likely to find them in the present system. Not only do the poor have the most limited financial resources, they have the most limited access to good information, to public transportation, to testing and counseling services. No matter where they turn, they must try twice as hard.

The Japanese, who boast one of the most successful school systems in the world, tell interviewers that they have the "best bottom half in the world." They do. They have perfected mass education, and educate nearly everyone. Americans once thought we could get by with the best "top half." We cannot, for both moral and practical reasons. Whose children should be left behind? The moral answer is that none need be left behind, none should be. We can all do it. And the practical answer is the same. We cannot afford to leave anyone behind. If we leave people behind, not only will their future be bleak, but so too will ours. And our great experiment of free markets and democracy will founder.

CHAPTER 3

Strategies for Reform

Education with inert ideas is not only useless; it is, above all things, harmful. . . . Every intellectual revolution which has ever stirred humanity into greatness has been a passionate protest against inert ideas.

—Alfred North Whitehead
The Aims of Education

In education as in life, practice precedes theory; experience precedes the abstract. This is the case with Next Century Schools, which build on demonstrated accomplishment in the real world; real teachers, real principals, real students in real communities solving real problems. And that is the lesson from school after school, in places as far removed from each other as the Recess Math Program in Oregon and the Ortega Elementary School in Austin, Texas; from Linda Vista Elementary in San Diego, California, to Piscataquis Community High School in the rural Appalachian highlands of western Maine. Piscataquis Community High School, for example, serves a largely working-class population in Guilford, Maine—a typical mill town. Today the mill is gone, and has been replaced by light manufacturing and diversified forest products. The more well-to-do students attend private schools, but the rest attend public schools. For years, Piscataquis Community High School was typical, of both Maine and the nation. It stressed vocational and business-related courses for most youngsters, and reserved a small number of challenging academic courses for the few students who showed great promise. Indeed, most of the teachers and students at Piscataquis thought this was a perfectly normal and proper thing to do, as do many Americans to this day. But an inventive principal and a few resourceful teachers were all that it took to break down the old barriers. The *Maine Sunday Telegram*'s September 15, 1991, issue describes a Piscataquis math teacher as follows:

> Rusty Sweeny, who mostly taught math to top students for much of his career, led the effort to dump general and business math in favor of solid math-skill courses for all. His students now work at individual levels. He roams the room, answering questions and keeping order, and is aided by four computers that guide students through sets of math problems. Students are at different levels, he said, but all are headed toward a well-entrenched, working knowledge of algebra. "No one fails in here," he said. "If they fail I have them try it again. I'm kind of like a pit bull."

Norm Higgins, Piscataquis's principal, credits Sweeny for persuading parents to embrace a new approach that requires higher standards for everyone. In a meeting attended by seventy parents—many of whom were themselves graduates of Piscataquis—Sweeny stood up and "in an emotional talk, apologized to them for the way the school had taught many of its students in the past. Sweeny becomes red with embarrassment when he is asked about that meeting now, but his feelings have not changed." When asked, Sweeny asserts, "The problem with education isn't that schools aren't what they used to be; the problem is that schools are what they used to be."

The example of Sweeny teaching serious algebra to everyone is more than an appealing story. It is based in part on serious research with which Higgins and his staff are familiar. In this case, it is a recent study by the College Board that revealed that students of all races and backgrounds who take both algebra and geometry are almost equally likely to attend college! In today's high-tech world, these are the gatekeeper courses for science, engineering, medicine and allied health fields, and computers. Without knowledge of algebra and geometry, today's student is tomorrow's failure.

Higgins's approach is not limited to math. English is offered the same way, with double periods and seminars on serious works of literature for all students. And he and his staff understand computers; there is no computer lab with the corresponding computer-literacy classes. Instead, computers are available in most classrooms—and in the library—where they are used for data display and management, word processing, and research. Higgins understands that computers are tools which provide intellectual leverage, in the same way a carpenter's hand tools provide mechanical leverage.

To provide a setting in which double periods have become the norm and in which demanding courses are expected of everyone, Higgins and his staff had to jettison general and vocational courses—long the mainstay of most high schools. It also meant prodigies of leadership and team building, a major change for a school that had been hierarchical and orderly. The shift in emphasis was revealed in a transformation noted by University of Maine professor Richard Babb. He dryly observed that when the initial retreat was held to kick off the Next Century School program, the staff referred to the RJR Nabisco grant as "Norm's grant." After the retreat they described it as "our grant." And it has become their grant. Working as a team they have transformed Piscataquis Community High School.

The Rappahannock County school system in Sperryville, Virginia, is composed of only two schools: an elementary building that also houses middle grades, and a high school.

Beneath its rural, small-town exterior, however, beats a steady rhythm of high technology and innovation, thanks in large measure to its superintendent, David Gangel. Gangel has brought big corporate support, advanced computer technology, and TQM techniques to his two-school district. The high school's traditional "shop" classes work on computer-aided design projects. Potomac Edison Power Company has made major investments in the schools, and 95 percent of all school system employees have been trained in total quality management. Gangel himself is a certified TQM trainer.

Clearly, David Gangel is an educator of many talents. However, these managerial and entrepreneurial skills aside, evaluators were stunned to learn of his other abilities. The Next Century Schools plan at Rappahannock is an effort to completely computerize the fourth grade curriculum. Inasmuch as the end result of this project will require students to spend a substantial portion of the school day at their computers, the plan calls for use of special fourth-grader-sized workstations to replace conventional desks. Commercial products were too expensive and "just not right." After a few unsuccessful attempts to use local people (including the high school CAD class) to come up with a design for the "desk," evaluators were pleased to learn that the school had been able to come up with a prototype workstation. How did they get the prototype produced? The superintendent spent a weekend in his home workshop drawing, sawing, and nailing together a model that would fit the Next Century Schools program specifications.

Gangel's ingenuity and resourcefulness has left program observers awestruck and more than a little envious of his job—a superintendency that affords him opportunities to both bring big things to a small district and simultaneously and quite literally have a hands-on approach to education.

How Should Schools Be Reformed?

Based on the experiences of Norm Higgins and Dave Gangel, as well as of other Next Century Schools and other innovators in public education, here are seven strategies that can make a difference for schools:

1. SET CLEAR GOALS, AND MEASURE PROGRESS TOWARD THEM.

Every successful organization has a clear sense of purpose: what it is and what it intends to accomplish. Except in the most vague and inconclusive way, public schools have failed to specify their goals. As a nation, and as individual communities, we must decide what we want our students to know and be able to do, and how our schools should deliver this knowledge. What minimum standards must all students achieve in each subject area, and how much are we willing to pay to ensure that each student reaches these targets?

The most important single decision a school community makes is what to teach. This is a critical and demanding issue, and encompasses two main aspects. One is the "visible" curriculum; the other, the "invisible." The visible curriculum is the academic content—standard written and spoken English, mathematics, history, geography, science, a second language, music, and art. The invisible curriculum is a school's expectations about demeanor and deportment, honesty, reliability, enterprise, courtesy, and attitude toward self, others, and work.

Neither curriculum is more important than the other; indeed, they are two sides of the same coin, and the most powerful tool to impart the one is the other. The great documents of citizenship play a central role in imparting both knowledge and attitudes, beginning with Plato's *Republic* and including Lincoln's *Second Inaugural,* as well as the *Declaration of Independence* and Martin Luther King's *Message from Birmingham Jail.* Equally important is the quality of the adults in contact with students; by their example teachers and other adults communicate to students the right values.

School goal-setting achieved national importance in 1989–90 when the nation's governors met with President George Bush in an historic education summit to begin the process at a national level. But we must reach far beyond these general national targets. Individual schools must adopt a detailed set of curriculum goals, linked to the evolving needs of society and the economy. At a minimum, these standards should include the ability to write clearly and speak persuasively in American English; competence in mathematics, including algebra and statistics; an understanding of the basic principles and applications of the physical and biological sciences and the scientific method; knowledge of geography and history; and the capacity to assemble evidence to solve problems. Defining national and state requirements in terms of years of math and English, rather than specific knowledge and competencies, no longer makes sense.

Next Century Schools first asked schools applying for support to define their goals. What do they intend to accomplish over the three years of the program? This step is often as important as winning the grant itself. For most schools the hardest and most useful task is to ask themselves the first question: What do we want to accomplish?

Piscataquis Community High School is an example of a school that works because it has set clearly defined goals for teachers and students; and these goals have implications. On the plus side of the ledger, everyone is expected to pursue a demanding course of study. Everyone is given the opportunity to learn; everyone is expected to. Reinforcement is the norm, not the exception. On the other side of the ledger, older, "easy" courses have simply been eliminated. There is no longer any place to "dump" low achievers or youngsters who are not highly motivated. Visit Rusty Sweeny's math class. A troubled student, one experiencing social as well as academic frustrations, is working quietly on a computer as he composes himself and catches up. When he's ready, he returns to the normal give-and-take of the classroom.

At the same time that schools set goals, they must measure their progress toward them. The business adage "What gets measured gets done" must be accepted by schools. Clear goals must be measured with unequivocal yardsticks. In particular, we must evaluate our schools with the same productivity focus that is used to measure efficiency in other areas. How much do students learn each month or year that they attend school? How great are these learning gains per dollar spent? How satisfied are the customers of education— parents and students—with the services they receive?

In simplest terms, the question schools must answer is, "What is the added value of schooling?" What difference does going to school make? Of course, students are not widgets, and education is not manufacturing. Many skills and competencies that we want our children to learn can only be measured with difficulty, or not at all, on standardized tests. But the complexity of the measurement task cannot be allowed to deter us from establishing specific standards. Despite the difficulties and risks, we need national tests that allow us to determine whether students have achieved targeted goals.

Beyond this measurement of school performance against absolute standards, school performance must be measured relative to other similarly situated schools. Firms constantly compare, or "benchmark," themselves against their competitors, both at home and abroad, as well as against noncompeting firms. Xerox, for example, compares itself to L.L. Bean for inventory control and to Florida Light and Power for customer-service response time. Schools should do no less. Wealthy suburban districts, for example, should not take satisfaction in comparing themselves to impoverished inner-city schools. Rather they should compare themselves to the best suburban districts, the best magnet schools, the best private schools, and then they should compare themselves to the competition: Berlin, Taipei, Seoul, Tokyo, Paris.

As well, we must be able to compare individuals against other students from similar socioeconomic and educational backgrounds to benchmark relative performance of individuals, schools, teachers, principals, and school systems.

2. FIND LEADERS, AND GIVE THEM RESPONSIBILITIES.

To survive and to progress, every organization needs strong leaders. Whether the task is leading a country, running a company, or managing the branch office, individual leaders must be able to define and describe a mission for their organization, motivate other people to share that mission, and stimulate action to realize it. Schools seldom search for principals with these characteristics. Instead, leadership is often actively discouraged by school systems. The system by which principals are selected should be changed to find and reward high-energy, high-performance people.

Rather than promoting those who have simply taken the requisite courses in schools of education or put in the required years in the classroom, we should seek people from inside and outside the system who have a demonstrated capacity to lead and manage people. Training programs for leaders, drawn from business models, should be implemented. Principals should be paid in some part based on the performance of their students and the satisfaction of their customers, including teachers, parents, and students.

One of the most striking lessons of Next Century Schools was the way leaders emerged in every successful school. Given the freedom to manage their own budgets, and the task of defining their own goals, most schools found individuals within the school who could realize the school's vision. In some cases, the leaders were individual teachers; in others the sparkplug was a supportive district official. In many circumstances, it was the principal who made the difference.

In case after case, Next Century Schools have demonstrated the truism that leadership matters. At University Terrace Elementary in Baton Rouge, Louisiana, Principal Steve Ketcham labors against enormous odds, from a high concentration of poverty to the ravages of Hurricane Andrew in the second year of the program. He is indefatigable and energetic, leading by example, exhortation, and enthusiasm. So is Principal Linda Tinsley at Ortega Elementary in Austin, Texas. Like most good principals, Linda's leadership "aura" spills over to other staff and parent volunteers, who are themselves infused with leadership capacities. When a terrified, gun-wielding dope addict tried to hide from "enforcers" on the school playground, parent volunteers and teachers instantly swung into action to shepherd children to safety and help mobilize the police. Indeed, the episode galvanized the community, and parents successfully petitioned the school board to finally fence the school grounds to protect the students from the adult drug culture in the neighborhood.

But in most large school bureaucracies, there is little room for leaders to emerge. Surrounded by specifications for textbooks, requirements for what, when, how much to teach, and rules and standards governing virtually every kind of activity, schools are trapped in red tape. Good people must have the authority and responsibility to do their jobs at the individual, school-building level. Because schools should be held accountable for their performance, virtually every decision about how to educate children should be made by the responsible teachers and staff. Hiring, firing, and most budget decisions should be made at the school level. How, when, and what to teach should be decided primarily by teachers. Similarly, the appropriate union bargaining unit is each school, rather than the school district or the state. Finally, the central office should become a service center, not a command center; the central office should have to "sell" its services to schools, not order them around. By this device the central office would have to pass a market test as well.

3. FIND TALENTED EMPLOYEES, INVEST IN THEM, AND REWARD THEM.

The heart of every organization is its staff. Schools treat teachers much as automobile companies used to treat assembly-line laborers—like cogs operating within large systems. The modern firm no longer treats employees as interchangeable parts, slowly depreciating as they age. To the contrary, a company's workforce is its most important asset, and as a workforce ages, it seasons and matures. It appreciates. A modern school's workforce is no different. The best schools recruit talent from virtually any source and deploy it in novel ways. These include not only teachers, but technology specialists, business leaders, architects, bankers, college professors, artists, journalists, public relations specialists, marketers, and other people schools have not traditionally employed. Some of the most successful Next Century Schools are those that had the freedom to hire new staff. At New Stanley Elementary in Kansas City, Kansas, and The Downtown School in Winston-Salem, North Carolina, for example, teachers were selected from applicants who applied from throughout the school district. These committed, engaged volunteers have made it possible to dramatically change the way these schools operate.

Once the talented employees are hired, they must be enabled to invest systematically in themselves. Teachers need time to collaborate with each other, to upgrade their styles and techniques of teaching, and to keep up with the advance of knowledge in their disciplines. Talented staff are revealed in small and large ways. The North Carolina School for Science and Mathematics, for example, is part of the University of North Carolina, not the state public school system (though it is a public school). As a consequence, NCSSM is not required by law to hire only certified teachers. As a result of that waiver, most of the teachers hired are not certified; they are former university and college teachers, practitioners, and professionals. Smart, dedicated, and capable, the NCSSM faculty looks much more like that of a private school than a typical public school. In a state which reports that there are only eleven people certified to teach high school physics, NCSSM's science faculty is almost all Ph.D.s!

By way of contrast, at Denali Elementary School in Fairbanks, Alaska, a Chapter One teacher's aide is a serious dog-musher. Every few days throughout the winter, she works with her six-dog team, no matter how bitterly cold the weather. And throughout the summer she cares for her dogs and mends harnesses and "booties" (today's dogs run with protective "foot gear"!). Although mushing is a sport, it is virtually a full-time job, yet she finds time to share her experiences with her students, taking them on rides in the Alaskan wilderness, reconnecting them to their own traditions, and demonstrating that there are no limits.

Virtually every Next Century School embarking on major reforms decided to use at least part of its grant to provide time and money for teachers to learn. In most cases, it was the teachers themselves who defined the courses. Some schools used training sessions to develop new courses, others sent teachers individually to seminars of their choice, and others brought in leading innovators or "change agents." All recognized that investment in their staff was a crucial part of the restructuring process.

Finally, talented, professional teachers must be paid as such. Today's schools are an anachronism in many ways, but in no way is this revealed more forcefully than in compensation practices. The best teachers and the worst teachers are paid the same; those in scarce disciplines are paid what those in abundant supply are paid. And incredibly, the best trained—professional mathematicians or linguists, for example—are not paid at all because they cannot be induced to take the mindless education courses required as a condition of certification. If they enter the classroom, they can only do so as guest lecturers—a certified teacher must be in attendance at all times. Paying for performance raises thorny questions of fairness and invites abuse. But the difficulty of the task should simply encourage administrators, teachers, and teacher associations to redouble efforts to find a solution that works. Paying the marginally fit, or worse yet, the unfit, the same as the best and brightest invites cynicism.

4. INVEST TO INCREASE SCHOOL PRODUCTIVITY.

In the larger economy, productivity growth has been the engine of prosperity. The analogy is clear: For the first time in history it should be possible to imagine educating everyone at expenditure levels which are reasonable and which will enjoy large-scale public support. The productivity of the modern economy that has enabled us to feed, clothe, and house nearly everyone adequately is based largely on human capital: the sum of the knowledge, skills, attitudes, dreams, insights, and institutions of the workforce. And the social institution that creates this human capital, at least the one institution amenable to policy influence, is the school. It is time, finally, to modernize the institution of the school to make it more productive and enable it to create more human capital with the same or fewer resources. The issue is not treating schools as a production process, but transforming a moribund institution into a highly productive one.

School budgets are still spent almost exclusively on salaries for teachers, administrators, and other school personnel. School capital budgets, which now focus primarily on buildings, should be aimed at tools and systems that can stretch the power of teachers to teach and to communicate: various technologies of communication and instruction, training, management, record-keeping, diagnostics, and testing. The goal should be fewer teacher-hours per unit of learning gain, and higher wages for people who are employed in school systems.

Most Next Century Schools include the use of technology as a part of their educational reform strategies. But only a few, typically those in partnership with business, see technology as a tool that can significantly increase the productivity of the school: that is, by increasing the rate at

75

which students learn, reducing the cost of instruction, or both.

Next Century Schools are technologically sophisticated, using technology as a tool, not a device for becoming "computer literate"—a process analogous to making students "automobile literate" as distinct from learning to drive. Knowing how a machine works is interesting but not essential. Knowing how to make a machine do your bidding *is* essential (as well as interesting). A few Next Century Schools, however, are poised to make major technological breakthroughs, with the probability of major productivity increases. For example, Rappahannock Elementary, which has embraced total quality management as well as technology, is fast approaching a point at which it can abandon conventional textbooks and rely exclusively on teacher-designed (and computerized) materials. Not only does the teacher-designed material promise lower costs, it promises higher output. The teachers know it and like it better; so do the students.

Productivity improvements should not be directed exclusively at cutting costs, however. Some types of schooling may cost more. For example, bringing the least advantaged students up to society's norms, with preschool, after-school, boarding school, social services, or other investments, is sure to be more expensive than today's school. Many Next Century Schools have allocated funds for these uses, considering such investments to be cost-effective when compared to the costs of welfare dependency, incarceration, and marginal employability that are the consequences of failure in school.

Still, while some aspects of education will be more expensive, no institution, public or private, escapes the responsibility to contain costs. Schools are no exception. Yet educators have insistently requested additional funds as the universal remedy to any problem confronting the schools. As a result, habits of cost containment often seem not to exist. The time has come for all to agree that money, while a part of the answer, is not the only answer.

What is counterproductive is to approach education as though the only solution to the problem of limited resources is more money. There are other solutions, including such obvious things as using parents and volunteers to assist teachers, or increasing class sizes in subjects where this is appropriate. Why, for example, is college physics taught to eighteen-year-olds in lectures of three hundred students, while high school physics is taught to seventeen-year-olds in classes of twenty-five?

Strategies to encourage more performance from students themselves, of course, have the highest payoffs. For example, some Next Century Schools have adopted cooperative learning strategies, where students teach other students, an approach that can raise the performance of both the student teacher and the student learner.

One area in which school productivity possibilities are particularly great is in the management of time: more effective utilization of buildings, people, and students. In modern economies, time has become increasingly valuable. Only in moribund economies, in which individual effort produces little of value, is time nearly "cost free." Yet schools are largely indifferent to the future use of time.

There are, in schools as well as other forms of social organization, four major aspects to the effective use of time, all of which are variations on one theme: time on task. Students learn what they study, so the more they study the better.

- *Uninterrupted study sessions:* Providing uninterrupted time on task is the most powerful learning technique at our disposal. It is the one policy variable that most sharply distinguishes American schools from the schools of our competitors. For example, as Michigan's Harold Stevenson reports in his studies of Japanese and Taiwanese schools, *The Learning Gap,* Japanese and Taiwanese youngsters spend much more time in the classroom on task than American students do.

- *Homework:* American students do much less homework than their foreign counterparts. Homework is essential, not just to keep kids out of trouble and to give them more time on task, but to create habits of self-directed study, one of the key traits for success in later life.

- *Length of the school day:* The American school day is simply not long enough for students to learn all that they must to succeed in the modern world. Lengthening the day need not be thought of exclusively in terms of increased labor costs or more teachers. Self-directed student learning, using modern computers, has a role; "study gangs" of the kind pioneered by University of California, Berkeley, mathematician Uri Treisman can be widely used, as can student mentors and tutors. The final report of the National Education Commission on Time and Learning will be available by September 1994, and will be an invaluable resource for schools that want to reconsider the use of time. The report will be available from the Commission in Washington, D.C., or through the Government Printing Office.

- *Length of the school year:* There is a reason the Japanese go to school 243 days a year: there is too much to learn in the modern world to pack it all into 180 days a year. Americans recognize this as a practical matter—half of our high school graduates go on to higher education. The Japanese attend school 243 days a year and have the equivalent in days alone of four years of college by the time they earn a high school diploma. A longer school year is not just more of the same. More time is particularly important for kids at risk because it can reduce or eliminate "summer learning loss."

More time in class, more homework, a longer day, and a longer year will mean that motivated and capable students will move through school more rapidly, graduating early or taking college-level work before their eighteenth birthday. This would represent a major productivity increase for the system as a whole, a breakthrough to be encouraged in the strongest possible terms.

Of the forty-two Next Century Schools, thirty-five have lengthened the time available for learning, through longer days, longer years, or Saturday sessions.

Like goal-setting, the search for productivity gains is not a one-time affair, but a continuous effort. The hallmark of the modern high-tech, high-performance firm is continuous improvement. A commitment to continuous improvement is a recognition that no static enterprise can long survive, and that there is no ultimate, right way to do it. Finally, continuous improvement means that workers are not production cogs in an indifferent machine, but valued employees who can contribute insight and advice to improved operations. Indeed, as most high-performance firms have discovered, the most fertile flow of ideas to improve productivity comes from workers in the field, not remote managers. Too many teachers are isolated workers, with little opportunity to talk among themselves or to influence school building practices or school district policies. Indeed, they are a school's greatest untapped resource, and should be drawn into a process of debate, discussion, and policy formulation as a way to improve schools.

5.   CREATE NEW RELATIONSHIPS AMONG SCHOOLS, PARENTS, AND COMMUNITIES.

Parents are the unutilized "labor force" of schooling. As their children's first teachers, parents should be taught to be teachers (at home and at school), and co-decisionmakers about school policy and programs. Schools should consciously market themselves to parents, treating them not only as workers, but also as primary customers. Parent satisfaction should be a school's primary goal. In fact, the well-run school will find that parents are frequently in classrooms, just as teachers are in homes. Communication links between parents and teachers will be pervasive and extensive.

A large majority of Next Century Schools have attempted to build new relationships with parents. At some Next Century Schools the process has used elaborate technology, such as voice mail and computer bulletin boards. At others, the process resembles grass-roots campaigning: Teachers go door-to-door to visit parents, and volunteers organize to create new connections between the parents and the schools.

One of the most striking realizations of teachers and principals at Next Century Schools was how much greater the burden of communication was than they had anticipated. Of course, as schools were selected from among thousands of competitors for large grants, they were naturally the object of intense media interest, and they were scrutinized by other schools. More basically, however, each of these schools realized that to build and sustain its success, it would be necessary to communicate much more intensively with parents, taxpayers, legislators, and others in the local community.

Communication should be second nature to schools; that is, in large measure, what they are all about. But few institutions in modern society are worse at communication than schools. Their message, insofar as they have one, is largely unknown outside of education circles. Indeed, the gulf of ignorance that separates schools, business, and communities is vast, and at times seems unbridgeable.

As Honeywell CEO Jim Renier points out, schools have slowly (and invisibly) assumed a greater and greater social service burden, but almost no one in the larger community is aware of the scope and weight of social programs. Renier argues that schools are no longer academic institutions— they are "social service institutions first, schools second." Furthermore, schools will not be able to meet their academic responsibilities until they are more fully supported in their social mission. The answer? Communicate, says Renier.

Rosman Elementary School is a case in point. Located in a small, rural mountain town in the southwest corner of North Carolina about forty miles south of Asheville, Rosman's population is between 420 and 450 children, depending on the time of year and whom you ask. One of just four elementary schools in Transylvania County, students' homes are widely scattered throughout the mountains. As a consequence, all Rosman students are bused to school. In no community is communication more important, nor is community involvement more highly valued or more difficult to pull off. Rosman's success is in part a product of careful planning, but like most ventures that make it, a real person is behind the plan. In Rosman, it's Exie Henson. A fixture in Rosman for more years than most people can remember, Exie is as energetic as she is venerable. Beloved by teachers and parents alike, Exie gives Rosman's carefully crafted plans the added push of personal attention, vast knowledge of the community, and a special enthusiasm that is unique to Exie.

In addition to Exie, teacher Mildred Dodson is both a personal success story and an inspiration to her students. At sixteen years of age, she dropped out of school to marry and raise a family. Sixteen years later, with three sons, she returned to a childhood dream: to become a teacher. She earned her GED in 1969, enrolled in a two-year elementary education program at a local college, and went to work as a teacher's assistant at Rosman in 1971. She earned her A.B. and taught at Rosman until last year before finally retiring—to enter a doctoral program. Both Exie and Mildred offer ample evidence that the old saw is true: Communicate in your client's language.

6. ENGAGE STUDENTS.

Ted Sizer, Brown University professor, head of the Essential Schools Network, and former Dean of the Harvard Graduate School of Education, notes that teachers often exonerate themselves from responsibility for the poor performance of their students with the explanation, "I taught it, but they didn't learn it." As Albert Shanker, President of the American Federation of Teachers, notes, that's like a salesman saying, "I sold it, but the customer didn't buy it." Nothing happens in school unless students want to learn. Indeed, students must be the primary workers in schools: They must make the effort to learn.

Yet much schooling seems irrelevant, boring, or pointless

to many students. Unless schools can engage students in the process and the excitement of learning, nothing happens. Every Next Century School has experimented with new strategies designed to engage students in learning. At New Stanley Elementary School in Kansas City, Kansas, all education has become based on mastery, and the only grades are "complete" and "in progress." The idea of failure, so damaging to the interest and engagement of slow-learning students, has been banished from the school.

New Stanley Elementary, housed in a pre–World War I building, engages students through the power of its program and the enthusiasm of its staff and parents. With an active parents' program, and a growing Hmong refugee population, New Stanley teachers were concerned about bringing this newest immigrant group into the life of the school. A unit on Hmong dress, cuisine, and dancing was the ticket, introducing New Stanley students to the newcomers in a way that was helpful and interesting to both.

New Stanley's story has had mixed results, however, revealing just how difficult the path to reform can be. Hoping to win a "replication" grant from RJR Nabisco after a successful three years as a Next Century School, New Stanley's parents, teachers, and students were sorely disappointed to not qualify. A hesitant school board, and weak central-office interest in New Stanley, made it impossible for New Stanley to find the support needed to qualify for replication funding. In response to their disappointment, however, New Stanley's principal, teachers, and parents confronted the board; the board has decided on its own initiative to continue the work begun at New Stanley. And New Stanley will continue to proudly call itself a Next Century School.

In other Next Century Schools, kids who have mastered the material teach others who have not. In some schools, technology for teaching students has been deployed or developed. Other schools build the curriculum around work, since the primary motivation of their students is to get well-paying jobs.

Other schools have changed the structure of school, keeping children with the same teachers and mentors for longer periods of the day, or through several grade levels, to promote more personal interaction and engagement between students and teachers. Many schools have become convinced that high-performance learning environments must be smaller, with smaller schools, or schools-within-schools breaking up the impersonal anonymity common in large schools and school systems.

These approaches all seek to change the way in which the student is treated, from the student who is acted upon (the product of an assembly line) to the student as a worker, actively engaged in his or her own achievement.

7. REWARD SUCCESS, PENALIZE FAILURE.

The most powerful stimulus for change in business is the discipline of the marketplace: When customers are satisfied, business increases; when they are unhappy, it falters, and eventually fails. The function of a market is to communicate and discipline. Markets exchange information about willing buyers and sellers, reward efficient and responsive sellers, and penalize slothful and unresponsive ones. For most American schools—particularly those that serve the poor—this discipline is missing. The poor are a captive audience. The well-to-do and motivated members of the working class can bail out of unresponsive public schools and buy into private schools, including low-cost inner-city Catholic and Lutheran schools, or they can move to the suburbs. But the poor have no such choice. They are trapped and must rely exclusively on the school's goodwill. The only way to guarantee that schools will become and remain internationally competitive is to challenge them with the spur of the market. Once a community sets standards for itself, resources must flow toward schools that perform well, and away from those that perform badly.

This principle should be applied to teachers, principals, schools, and school systems. The formula need not be restricted to "choice" systems—allowing parents to choose where to send their children—but could include teacher rewards for superior performance or elements of privatization, such as contracting with Berlitz to teach foreign languages. At a minimum, high-performance schools, those that are benchmarked against schools with similar students, should receive special rewards and resources to expand. And the poorest performers should be declared intellectually and administratively bankrupt and put into receivership or out to bid. At the same time, school budgets and teacher pay should be tied to learning gains and to the measured satisfaction of parents and students.

A part of rewarding success and penalizing failure is the recognition that schools must be allowed to specialize. Successful schools cannot expect to be all things to all people; they must find a niche. Any organization can do one, two, or three things well. Few can do more than that. Schools, no less than other organizations, should identify what their strengths are, build on those, and present themselves as institutions that can deliver these promises.

Decentralization is the reciprocal of finding a niche. Unlike industries which produce high volumes of uniform products, education is a highly specialized and labor-intensive industry. The techniques and approaches to successful learning must vary depending on the background and learning styles of students, the subject, the age of the students, the community, and other factors. In schooling, the rule should be: To succeed, differentiate.

One little-noted aspect of private schooling has a direct bearing on this; the nation has approximately 21,000 private schools, yet of those no more than two dozen enroll more than 1,000 students. Why? Because private school administrators know that there are no economies of scale in education. To the contrary: In education, small is beautiful. Among Next Century Schools, at least a third have chosen to break their school into smaller, more personalized units. None have sought to enlarge classes or total enrollments.

Recently, the Foundation found itself in the disquieting position of being asked to renew an award to a school that couldn't—or wouldn't—live up to the terms and conditions of the original award. Sad to say, the temptation in any organization is to look away, hope the problem will resolve itself or go away altogether. With a time-limited grant the temptation is all the stronger. But we were convinced that no signal would be more dangerous—let a grantee think it can get away with failure to perform, and fail it will. Even more important, it sends a signal to other grantees: The Foundation isn't serious. Most important, it sends a dreadful signal to those who work hardest—and finally succeed against the odds: What you do doesn't make a difference. Good, bad, indifferent, you still get your grant.

Note the unhappy fact that this syndrome is not confined to grants and awards—it describes the whole system we call public education. The best teachers are paid what the worst are paid—so too, the worst are paid what the best are paid. And in only a few districts out of 15,700 across the nation are there any penalties for failure. Schools that fail continue to be funded. Indeed, in one of life's greatest ironies, it is often the school that fails that gets the most money!

The Foundation was determined not to fall into this trap, and has maintained a "watch list" and keeps grantees under close observation. Not to intimidate or hamper them—the purpose of the grants is "venture capital" to encourage entrepreneurship—but to be certain that they walk the walk, not just talk the talk. One school—Dunbar High School in Baltimore—had its funds cut off in midstream for a variety of reasons. Dunbar was unable to meet the targets it had set for itself as a grant condition. An even more striking example was a Next Century Schools award made to District of Columbia Public Schools to create a math-science high school for the city. Designed to look like the North Carolina School for Science and Mathematics (with no residential component), the Washington proposal was one of the strongest and most compelling submitted to the Foundation. Awarded $750,000 in the first year of the competition, the D.C. schools never picked up the check. Paralyzed by indecision, the fate of Mayor Barry (who was then facing legal action), and the fate of the superintendent (who was fired immediately after the subsequent school board election), the school board was unable to take decisive action and establish the math-science school.

What is one to make of these developments? It is tempting to think they are idiosyncratic, or signs of decay, venality, or stupidity—or all of the above. Indeed, they may be. But there is a much larger lesson to be learned. Even with money, and lots of it, true reform is hard to bring off. That's precisely why venture capital is needed. Even in the best of circumstances, change is difficult, fraught with peril, something most organizations would rather do without.

Taking Action: The Special Role of Business

Even if there were total agreement on the preceding seven points, education will not be reformed unless there is powerful pressure for change from outside the schools. Although Next Century Schools and other education reform efforts have found thousands of dedicated teachers and principals, these would-be reformers are virtually powerless to effect change from within.

Since change threatens vested interests, it is difficult to implement even by the most well-intentioned school bureaucracies. Pressure must be applied from outside the system. In theory, three sources of leverage could work on the public schools: the federal government, state governments, and business. However, the federal and state government are hamstrung by politics, budgets, and inertia.

The federal government, even though it supplies less than 6 percent of school resources, could theoretically demand that local schools and districts substantially reform their approach and strategies in education. For example, it would be relatively straightforward to tie federal assistance to disadvantaged students to systems that would require goal-setting, performance measurement, school-based management, and other basic reforms. Federal intervention of this kind, however, is not likely. Federal deficits place sharp limits on Washington's ability to "buy" change in the schools, even if it were so inclined. Moreover, the constitutional division of power in Washington between the White House and Congress makes it especially difficult to reach consensus to set a national agenda for public schools. The executive branch may propose, but Congress disposes. By virtue of size, tradition, and history, the Congress is not likely to produce legislation that will lead to wholesale restructuring of the nation's schools. Washington's education policies are trapped in intricate webs of special interest politics, budgetary limits, and bureaucratic inertia. As a consequence, looking to Washington (particularly to Congress) for leadership is not an encouraging prospect.

What is true of Congress is true of most state legislatures as well. While any state has the power to force basic change on its schools, through the leverage of state statute and funding, little has happened on this front. With the exception of a few states with particularly vigorous and determined governors or energetic legislators, few meaningful reforms in public education have originated in the statehouse. And even the most determined governors face a daunting array of enemies of reform. Indeed, to the reform-minded governor, the political landscape looks as though it is all checks and no balances, all barriers and no opportunities. Affected officials face an endless parade of special pleaders and special interests, all organized to maintain and protect the status quo. They have the organization, the resources, the energy, the trained staff, the intellectual horsepower to challenge the governor at every turn.

The issue is more than unions and professional associations; it is endemic and threatens the political process in its entirety. But the issue is specially acute when it is framed in terms of haves and have-nots. Put bluntly, the have-nots have no lobbyists, and they can triumph only if they have an enthusiastic champion. The governor who takes on a major issue like school restructuring finds he or she has few friends and countless enemies, at least in the beginning. Reform requires prodigious effort, and a willingness to spend political capital at a great rate.

Even parents, who might be assumed to be natural allies of reformers, are often an obstacle. Frequently they will oppose important reforms, such as year-round schools, because they are fearful about calendar changes that might affect family vacation plans.

Who are a governor's natural allies in the slow, hard work of education renewal? The public at large—most parents and children, if they understand the issues; but the capacity to mobilize them is limited, because they are a fragmented and disparate group. There is one segment of the population which cares about education and is not a member of a special interest group, at least in regard to education: business. Business cares about education for precisely the same reason the rest of the nation at large does, and business—in this case, at least—is not a special pleader, asking for favors or protection.

To the contrary, the business interest is simply in having an educated citizenry that can take its place alongside the world's best workforces. In this connection it is worth emphasizing that business is not interested in the creation of a docile and pliant workforce, made up of interchangeable parts—the exaggerated view of the industrial era's workforce. The workforce of the high-performance organization in the global economy is one that must be made up of autonomous problem-solvers, men and women who can think for themselves, reason and troubleshoot, and continue learning on the job. Modern workers are not interchangeable parts, which, like their industrial analogues, depreciate with age and use. They are workers who appreciate as they mature and learn more. When the workforce is understood in this light, the needs of business and society as a whole are drawn together. The historic mission of the school—to educate the whole person, not just the prospective job-seeker—is now precisely what is needed for employment in the modern world.

Business, then, is not only a major stakeholder in the issue of education quality, it is the only potential source of major institutional pressure on the system. Without business pressure to improve the schools there will be no one else to act. And if no one acts, the schools will ultimately fail to change, and fail to prepare our students and citizens adequately for the next century.

If business must act to force change, what should it do? On the one hand, business leaders have wrung their hands and issued stirring rhetoric; this is the impulse that leads to "adopt-a-school" programs. If that is all business does, it is not worth much. If it is the first step in a process of involvement, however, it can be invaluable.

The process of involvement requires business to take a page from its own book. What is business's comparative advantage as it looks at education? What does business know, and what can it do, to make a difference? Business has much to offer schools.

First and foremost (more so than even money), is a way of thinking, of viewing the world. Business must ask schools the questions they ask themselves: Who are your customers? What is the most efficient way to deliver the goods or services they want and need? What organizational system is best suited to deliver those services? What is your market "niche," or put slightly differently, what are you good at doing? How do you recruit, train, and compensate your employees? Do you reward high performance and extra effort? Do you let slackers get away with poor performance, accepting the demoralizing effect this has on other workers and customers? How do you use time? Is your physical plant scheduled for optimal usage? Is cost containment an integral part of everything you do, not to save money for its own sake, but to free resources for higher and better use? What roles does technology play in your organization? Is it simply bells and whistles, or is technology a fundamental part of your strategic plan to increase productivity?

Business has a special responsibility to help, both with its ideas and with its insistence on a businesslike approach to the national school problem. As one of the primary customers of the education system, which, after all, supplies most of the American workforce, business cannot afford to wait for the problem to fix itself gradually over the next several decades as parents and communities gradually wake up to the challenge and opportunities. Business must be a united voice for radical change now.

Management guru and prophet Peter Drucker, in *Innovation and Entrepreneurship: Practice and Principles,* captures the essence of the problem:

> The public school in the United States exemplifies both the opportunity and the dangers. Unless it takes the lead in innovation it is unlikely to survive this century, except as a school for the minorities in the slums. For the first time in its history, the United States faces the threat of class structure in education in which all but the very poor remain outside of the public school system—at least in the cities and suburbs where most of the population lives. And this will squarely be the fault of the public school itself because what is needed to reform the public school is already known.

CHAPTER 4

Goals Set, Goals Met

If you do not know where you are going, any road will take you.

—Unknown

If public schools are to reclaim their legacy they must return to their first principles. They must set new goals for the twenty-first century. Schools must set goals because goals reveal the reason an organization exists, and set the course the organization intends to follow. Without goals, an organization is rudderless and lacks the vision that motivates individuals to work together for a common purpose. Without clear goals, public schools drift in a sea of competing claims and pressures, accomplishing little. What are a school's goals? The identification of what students should know and be able to do, and how the school will achieve these ends. Everything else the school does must serve these purposes.

Unfortunately, most U.S. public schools still have many of the same goals they had when they were established in the nineteenth century. Indeed, most schools have failed to systematically reconsider what they are about. For instance, schools still operate on a calendar that was originally designed to release children to tend the crops. Schools still teach with tools and techniques that were familiar to Abraham Lincoln, and they often ignore subjects that have become indispensable in modern industry, such as statistics or business English.

Schools fail to reassess their goals and reorient programs not because of ill-will or intransigence, but simply because of inertia. They do not change their goals because they are not forced to. As protected bureaucracies, they are isolated from the pressures that force other institutions to change, particularly institutions that must serve customers in an open market.

Organizations that face changing markets and changing circumstances recognize that the process of setting goals is crucial to long-term success and survival. Corporations invest enormous effort and time in the complicated and often painful process of setting and resetting their goals. In modern organizations, setting specific goals is part of an elaborate and regular planning process. Annually, senior executives closet themselves to review trends and competitive conditions and to debate alternatives, finally emerging with a set of corporate goals and plans.

This process enables the group to define more effectively what it wants to accomplish and to then accomplish it. Structured goal-setting forces an organization to ask basic questions about what it is doing, and where it wants to go. By opening the process to many people, goal-setting can ensure that nearly everyone shares the institutional vision and will act together to realize it. Furthermore, by repeating the process every few years, an organization can adapt to changing circumstances or even radically change its mission.

For example, when the S.S. Kresge Company faced declining business as a traditional retailer, it undertook a searching reexamination of its goals and markets. Many people from inside and outside the company were involved in this process. As a result, Kresge undertook a fundamental makeover of the organization and its strategies, reemerging as the company known today as K Mart.

Such fundamental reexamination of basic goals rarely occurs in public schools because the process of setting goals is more confused, remote, and unfocused. In fact, schools themselves seldom set their own goals, or make plans for how to realize them. A school's goals are often set with little participation from the principal, teachers, parents, or students. The goals are usually established by an invisible assembly of pressure groups, bureaucrats, politicians, and officials. As a result, a school's mission most often emerges from an uncoordinated, and even unarticulated, process. Teachers, students, and parents come to understand the school's goals only when they are made visible in the numbing rigidity of required instruction, textbook prescriptions, and teacher certifications.

Any teacher who has sought to change textbooks, or parent who has tried to influence the school's curriculum, knows that this remote goal-setting process leaves schools with little power to make their own choices. The process is so distant, and the role of each individual so small, that virtually no one within an individual school believes that he or she has the power to affect a school's goals or the ability to revise plans that have been established by the authorities. What is even more damaging is that teachers, parents, and children typically feel no sense of ownership or even belief in their school's goals. Because teachers, parents, and children take no part in setting goals, no team forms to work together to achieve goals. As a result, most members of the school community feel they are simply carrying out orders. This "cogs-in-the-machine" psychology is particularly pervasive in large school districts where creative or energetic teachers often feel they must be outlaws, rather than committed disciples.

Any organization that does not periodically reestablish its

goals and recommit its members to their realization, is in danger of ultimately failing. Communism in the former Soviet Union, where few dared to ask basic questions, ultimately crumbled because no process existed to redefine the society's goals and rededicate its members to their realization.

Goal-setting must, of necessity, be a local process, reflecting local strengths and resources, as well as local attentiveness to the realities of a global economy and our shared national life. The range of schools among those funded by Next Century Schools is emblematic of the range among the schools in the nation funded as a whole, each with a distinctive personality, each with distinctive as well as common needs. Rancho Viejo Elementary School, for example, in the southwestern desert, serves a poverty-stricken population which is largely Hispanic, and so dispersed that "normal" school visits are a rarity—no surprise in a school district as big as a small Eastern state. To remedy the problem, Rancho Viejo received funds to outfit a "jumpstart" bus—a mobile classroom that brings education to parents, students who are enrolled in school, and preschoolers. Reminiscent of the bookmobiles of the 1950s, or the agricultural extension service of the past century, Rancho Viejo's program delivers the service where the customer is. A lively forty-nine-year-old grandmother shared this story with one of the teachers: Like her daughter and granddaughters, she thought she was too "dumb" to learn, and hesitated to even visit the bus. But she succumbed. She has learned to write her name, no small triumph, and she—and her daughter—now insist that the granddaughters attend school regularly. Rancho Viejo is the same as other schools, but their delivery is unique.

Greenburg Eleven Elementary School could not be more different. A public residential facility for deeply troubled youngsters from New York City, it serves students whose parents are abusive drug users or common criminals. Clearly the needs of these youngsters are very different from those of advantaged suburban youngsters or the rural poor—and the residential program reflects that. But at the same time the kids at Greenburg Eleven Elementary will need to make their way in an adult world, and to do so they will have to master the skills that all youngsters will need to compete in the twenty-first century.

Goal-setting cannot be accomplished from the top down. While it is fine for the nation to set goals for its education system, as President Bush and the nation's governors did in 1989, national goals cannot take the place of school-by-school goal-setting. National goals are general statements of principle and guides for national policymaking. Only local communities and individual schools can decide exactly what and exactly how they want to teach children.

When the RJR Nabisco Foundation offered Next Century School grants to individual public schools, it insisted that they set their own goals. For many schools, the process of goal-setting that preceded their application for a grant was a new, exciting, and unsettling process. They were forced to ask themselves three basic questions:

- What if we didn't have to obey district guidelines or live within district budgets, but could make our own plans?

- What are the main problems at our schools, and how can we fix them?

- Since we will be judged by our results, what are we better off spending money on: computers, teacher training, parent involvement?

Schools that won grants, and even those that did not, found that asking questions like these forced them to confront issues that they had ignored before. For example, many schools concluded that they lacked the knowledge to redesign their educational approaches. Juanita Elementary School in Kirkland, Washington, a 1992 winner, instructed its core team of planners to study educational reform efforts taking place across the country before beginning the goal-setting process. Other schools realized that in order to help the most poorly performing students, they would need a new array of relationships with parents, social service providers, and the community.

Vaughn Street Elementary School in San Fernando, California, decided that it needed an on-site health clinic to provide for the needs of its mostly minority population. Many schools realized that to raise test scores they would need to find ways to improve their teaching strategies and relationships with individual students. At Chelsea High School outside Boston, teachers created a Pathways school that operates in the afternoons and evenings to reach students who must work or attend drug rehabilitation sessions during the day.

For most schools, goal-setting was an exciting process that brought together people who earlier had not talked to each other at all. Even among schools that did not win, the process often triggered action and released energy that had not been possible before. One school that reached the finals in 1990 reported two years later that the process of goal-setting for the grant application "began a series of fundamental changes in the school that are still taking place today."

In some cases, goal-setting took place within the context of the creation of a brand-new school, allowing innovators to think about new ways of teaching, new standards for students, new systems of instruction, a new curriculum. At New Stanley Elementary School, for example, a new cadre of teachers set out to design and implement a school that would banish failure. This required teams of teachers working together, a new system of grading, a new, more participative management approach, and a much more intensive relationship with parents.

At other schools, the goal-setting process simply reestablished their commitment to long-recognized principles. At Morgan County Primary School in Madison, Georgia, the teachers and principal focused solely on the challenge of involving parents in the education of their K-2 children. As a result, the school developed an extensive, individualized program for bringing school to parents, and parents to the school.

This example illustrates the indispensable role that localized goal-setting plays in implementing national objectives. At the national level, the first goal enumerated by President Bush and the governors in 1990 was: "All children in America will start school ready to learn." But only a searching, grass-roots process at Morgan County Elementary could lead to the concrete goals and plans that will be needed to engage Madison parents in the preparation and education of their primary-age children.

The relationship between national and local goal-setting in Madison also illustrates another feature of successful goal-setting. To be effective, the process must involve a very wide array of people. Although not everyone will be involved at every stage or at the same time, principals, teachers, parents, and students must all participate if a school is to succeed.

The experience of various Next Century Schools illustrates how the process works. When Bloomfield Hills, an affluent community in Michigan, set out to develop a new model high school, it began the goal-setting process with a small group of teachers and counselors. As plans and ideas developed, the planners undertook an intensive series of meetings with parents, students, teachers, local businesses, and district officials. By the time the school won a Next Century Schools grant and opened a new school, the designers of the reforms had engaged hundreds of people from the school and the community.

At New Stanley Elementary, the goal-setting process involved teachers taking responsibility for their own and their school's progress. "What must we do," the principal, Donna Hardy, asked the teachers, "to improve our teaching strategies to reach more children more successfully?" The teachers gave answers in terms of the training they needed, the additional planning time they should spend together, the curriculum, and their relationships with parents. Because teachers set their own agenda, they take personal responsibility for the outcome of their personal and group development.

Stripped to its essentials, goal-setting is a way of directly engaging all the members of an organization in its mission, and of defining a plan for their personal participation in its success. It is the first step in a participative management process that delegates power to the workforce. In the case of schools, this workforce consists of both teachers and students.

A goal-setting process that includes many people is a revolution in the way the school and the school district operate. Goals that emerge from the bottom up, and that lead to actions throughout an organization, represent a fundamental restructuring of the way traditionally hierarchical schools govern themselves. Principals, superintendents, state bureaucrats, and others used to dictating plans must give up the power they have wielded. In asking all the individuals in the school about what they want accomplished, administrators are forced to listen to the answers. This can be the beginning of basic change in a school.

These divergent examples demonstrate that goal-setting may involve many different kinds of issues, in addition to the basic objective of improving student academic performance. Schools have found that they must target not only curriculum, but teaching strategies, school atmosphere, relationships among teachers, management styles, and many other variables in the school equation. Still others use goal-setting to rearrange the traditional times, places, and targets of schooling. Many NCS schools have lengthened the school day, extended programs year-round, and included the teaching of parents as one of their goals.

Setting Standards, Measuring Results

By itself, however, the process of setting goals can become an empty exercise, unless it is backed up by an explicit plan for action, a set of benchmarks of progress, and a system of measuring progress toward these goals. The difference between a productive group and one that is wasting everyone's time depends on whether the meetings close with explicit agreements on plans, assignments, and timetables for further action. So too with goal-setting. General goals must be made concrete and action-oriented, and then tied to certain expected results. Finally, there must be agreement on how success will be defined and measured.

The Duke Ellington School of the Arts in Washington, D.C., known across the country for its program, not just its namesake, offers a perfect example of standard-setting and results measurement—as the arts in general do. Standards are set by outstanding performers—dancers, musicians, actors, poets—and they are tested and demonstrated in auditions, frequently "blind." On occasion, aspiring musicians actually present out of sight of judges, who make determinations about technical accomplishment and artistic expression without being able to see the performers. Whether or not the practice is applied literally, the notion is a good one, both for admission to the program and for evidence of accomplishment. The next step: to develop portfolios that demonstrate accomplishment in fields other than the arts. And the arts will be a big player in the process used to help create the portfolios. Imagine students with a CD Rom disk with a complete student record; not just letter grades, but examples of work—essays, themes, research papers. Or examples of extracurricular activity: marching band or football in living color and sound. Or examples of editorials or articles in the student newspaper, video footage of lab work, or video footage of community service. The sky's the limit.

In business, where most things can be measured in dollars, the definition of success and the measurement of results may seem relatively simple. Did sales and profits rise as a result of the actions of the organization?

Business managers have learned, however, that the accurate measurement of performance is far more complicated, and that it is crucial to measure the right things in the right way, if the organization is to guide itself to continuous success. When a business measures the wrong things, or fails to measure the important things, it can lead to great gaps and failures in business performance.

For example, many businesses have been criticized for their failure to manage for long-term gains rather than short-term profits. But when managers are compensated primarily on annual improvements in profits, the incentive to invest for the long-term can be undermined. Similarly, many U.S. manufacturing companies have discovered themselves falling behind international competitors, after years of dominating U.S. markets. They have realized that their planning and measurement systems were comparing themselves to the wrong standards, (i.e., solely to U.S. competitors) and as a result they were setting their goals too low.

Now, the top U.S. firms routinely measure their performance against the best in the world, and set their goals at or above these levels. More importantly, these firms now seek to improve their performance continuously, regardless of where they stand in world competition. This philosophy, which demands that the company always use itself as a benchmark, and strive to improve on its previous performance, is the basis of modern management. Since success is defined as improvement in the statistical indices tracked by managers, it is crucial for firms to choose the right things to measure.

Schools face similar challenges. At one level, the measurement of the results of schooling seems as simple as the task of measuring a firm's profits. Have standardized achievement test scores risen as a result of the actions taken by the school? But as anyone who has explored the subject of standards and testing realizes, setting explicit standards for schools and measuring their results is anything but straightforward.

Any suggestion for standards and tests to measure progress is quickly met by a chorus of criticism from teachers, parents, and students. For example, when the National Council on Education Standards and Testing recommended in early 1992 that there be a set of voluntary national standardized tests administered to students in the fourth, eighth, and twelfth grades in English, mathematics, history, geography, and science, there was an immediate barrage of objections from, among others, the heads of the nation's teacher unions, and from such highly regarded education reformers as Ted Sizer.

It would be easy to categorize some of these criticisms as reluctance to be held accountable, coming from professional educators who are afraid that they may not measure up. But the criticism of standard-setting and testing deserves closer scrutiny. Next Century School principals and teachers—all dedicated innovators willing to be judged on their results— agree that current testing leaves much to be desired; better instruments to measure progress must be developed.

There are four main arguments against national standardized testing:

- National tests will dictate a national curriculum, and will prevent the kind of bottom-up goal-setting needed to improve schools at the local level.

- Current generations of standardized tests measure rote knowledge and ignore many competencies that are as important (for example, creative or artistic talents), while encouraging unimaginative, boring approaches to learning.

- Standardized tests are unconnected with the subjects being taught, and provide little guidance to teachers as to what they should do to improve the performance of their students.

- Current standardized tests are culturally biased, and brand too many students as failures, especially minorities. By creating so much failure, they become self-fulfilling prophecies that reinforce failure in students that perform poorly.

To each of these critiques there are rebuttals. Will national standards dictate a national curriculum? There is already a *de facto* national curriculum, in terms of years of English, required mathematics, sciences, U.S. history, and other subjects, at least for college entry. Moreover, most Americans agree that proficiency in English and mathematics and knowledge of history and science are indispensable prerequisites for informed citizenship and productive work.

As for the presumed rigidity and misdirected focus of current multiple-choice tests, test designers have experimented with other forms of tests, such as those that measure performance in work-related skills (for example, writing a business letter asking for a job, or giving a presentation describing a product for sale). Such tests are more time-consuming and expensive to administer, and have their own weaknesses. And cultural bias is hard to determine. Elaborate efforts to create tests without cultural bias do not necessarily raise the scores of minority test-takers. A multiyear effort to create a racially neutral, job-related promotional exam in the New York City Police Department, for example, resulted in fewer high minority scores than the test it replaced. Most important, as E. D. Hirsch and others argue, our schools are supposed to transmit and reinforce "cultural literacy."

Finally, the issue of the impact of low test scores on students' self-esteem and teacher expectations must be dealt with by addressing the ways in which students are taught and expectations set, rather than by abandoning tests and standards. At New Stanley Elementary School, the teachers have wholeheartedly adopted the philosophy that "All children can learn." Here, educators work hard to remove the idea of failure from the language and practice of both students and their teachers. Since all students are expected to master certain material, there are only two levels of achievement: mastered and incomplete. While some students may take longer, and require more help to master the material, they are never judged to have failed, but are assumed simply to be continuing to work to achieve the objective.

Of course, truly putting this philosophy into practice requires schools to tailor their educational approaches much more to the individual student, and to be willing to invest more time and resources in slow-learning students. But schools adopting this approach emphatically do not quit testing students, nor do they lower standards to accommodate slower learners. Indeed, they may test constantly to encourage incremental progress, and raise standards as they improve student performance. At New Stanley the goal is that *every* child will be at or above grade level.

Understood in this context of high expectations and positive reinforcement, the risks of testing and tough standards are less threatening. To be defined as successes, all students do not need to master material immediately. They simply need to keep trying. One afternoon at New Stanley Elementary, Principal Donna Hardy took time out to congratulate a fifth-grader on his recent success on a math exam. The boy accepted her encouragement with a beaming smile. "He told me he was so happy after passing, that he couldn't sleep last night," she remarked. The test, which had required the boy to correctly answer twenty-nine of thirty multiplication questions from flash cards, had been easily mastered by his classmates weeks earlier. Yet instead of being left behind, and crushed by a sense of failure, the youth was delighted with his long-delayed success. Tests, and high standards, do not have to lead to more failure among slower students.

Despite these rebuttals, it is clear that current generations of tests do not satisfy educators, and are not as useful or accurate as they could be. Just as it is crucial for businesses to set the right goals, and to measure progress against the right standards, so it is important for schools to measure progress soundly. After all, the main reason for creating testing and measurement systems is to improve the performance of schools and their students.

Although tests may also be used to sort students according to ability, to allocate further educational opportunities, or to reward outstanding individuals, the main purpose of a system of testing is to guide the management of the educational system so that it can maximize the "educational productivity" of young learners and their teachers. If tests have the effect of discouraging some students from trying hard, or of inhibiting curiosity and creativity, or of preventing schools from establishing their own goals, then the tests deserve skeptical scrutiny, and possible modification.

But skeptical scrutiny is not the same as blanket rejection. If schools are to advance, there must be clear standards and continuous measurement of progress. How should this be done, especially in light of the criticisms of educators?

The "right" tests for American schools will have these characteristics:

- They will inform students, parents, and teachers how well each individual has mastered specific educational goals, including both understanding of bodies of knowledge and acquisition of skills. These measurements will be set against a continuous scale of mastery, not defined by grade levels.

109

- They will inform teachers about both the knowledge their students have acquired, and their own performance as teachers compared to teachers of similar students.

- They will enable comparisons of individual students, teachers, schools, districts, and nations. These comparisons will be benchmarked against equivalent students, schools, or nations, and against "expected" outcomes. For example, tests should permit comparisons between Montgomery County, Maryland, and students in similar high-income communities worldwide.

- They should provide prompt, continuous feedback to teachers and students, including specific recommended educational strategies to improve their performance.

- They should be inexpensive, both in terms of their direct costs and the time devoted to tests by teachers, graders, and students.

Obviously, current testing systems fall far short of these goals. Some of the current limitations are self-imposed. For example, there has been little effort to cross-validate and cross-reference various standardized tests (e.g., to correlate scores on one test with those on another). No single national test is taken by every student. For various reasons, politicians, test-makers, educators, and others have combined to block comparisons between students, schools, and districts. In some cases, the resistance stems from legitimate fears that the comparisons would be unfairly interpreted; in others, it appears that test-marketers are reluctant to undercut sales of proprietary products by accepting standardization.

Most importantly, tests have not been calibrated against a fair set of expectations. Throughout the nation, the "Lake Woebegone" effect dominates, in which every child is "above average." Only in a few, visionary school districts, like Charlotte-Mecklenburg, North Carolina, are scores reported to parents to inform them how their children are doing, both compared to children from similar backgrounds, and compared to what would be expected based on their child's previous performance in school. And producers of standardized tests seldom produce "criterion-referenced tests," linked to specific curricula, teaching strategies, or other educational approaches. Yet at the same time, most educators correctly complain that tests already take too much time away from teaching, and cost too much money. Charlotte's use of criterion-referenced tests and school-building "report cards" is a major breakthrough that other districts across the country should emulate.

Obviously, the development of a satisfactory testing system to guide education reform will require many years and millions of dollars. Not only must there be broad national agreement over education goals, there must be elaborate development of standards and benchmarks to measure progress. If one test is not to be adopted by all, then at least all standardized tests must be comparable to each other.

Moreover, ideal tests will need to be embedded in teaching tools and administered by computers in relatively short periods of time. For example, a computerized test can select from thousands of test items—questions to quickly probe the limits of a student's knowledge and provide a highly accurate picture of skill development in many areas. Regular, brief tests in such a system can provide accurate and useful scores—in various competencies—for each student. Once the testing data is on the computer, it is relatively simple to provide comparisons, benchmarks, and instructional guidance to the student, to his or her parents, and to teachers.

Alternatively, as more instruction is delivered *via* interactive computers, the computer tracks how well and how fast each student masters the material. The computer becomes a diagnostic and reporting tool, not just a teaching machine.

Finally, for some types of skills it will be necessary to develop standardized performance tests: for example, writing a job application letter; giving a verbal defense before a panel; organizing a group of people to accomplish a task; planning and scheduling to achieve an objective; searching for the appropriate information to answer a question; or teaching someone else what you have just learned. Tests to measure these skills will provide more accurate indicators for responsible citizens and productive employees.

But the current lack of valid, fully-developed tests should not deter educators from insisting on more extensive and consistent use of tests. Although poorly designed tests may mislead, the bigger risk is to avoid tests and comparisons altogether. Better a weak test than no tests.

Until tests are available that enable parents and students to understand what is happening at school and to inform teachers and school administrators on how well schools and students are performing, education will be unable to improve substantially. In communist economies, the absence of real prices and wages kept resources from going to where they were needed, and prevented development of more efficient production processes. Education without adequate tests lacks guidance on how to improve. With no benchmarks, educators will continue to wander in the forest of reforms, taking first one road and then another, without ever knowing what works.

The complexities of measuring progress, or the constraints of state or federal mandates, should not be allowed to deter reformers from taking action in local schools. The first, most urgent step is for parents, teachers, and principals to set goals for their school. Once this process has been undertaken, and expanded to reach large numbers of those involved with a school, it can become a powerful lever for change. Whether the goals are a restatement of challenges the school has already been addressing, or a dramatic shift of direction and attention, the process of unifying the school behind a plan of action is an indispensable first step in the achievement of a new, higher level of performance.

The question of testing and measurement inevitably brings up the question of self-esteem. We are convinced that it is important, but that it cannot be conferred. It must be earned, the old-fashioned way, by hard work. But habits of hard work, even the opportunity to work hard, and encouragement and rewards for hard work are unevenly distributed. The gifted football player, dancer, musician, or tennis player will frequently find that rewards for hard work are numerous, perhaps too numerous. The LaGuardia School of the Performing Arts in New York City has a hard time graduating male ballet dancers because by the time they are seventeen or eighteen years old, they are so good that they are ready to go straight to Broadway. But that's a "better" problem than the one that often occurs at the other end, where school begins. What of the talented and enterprising youngster who is too shy, too poorly informed, or too far from the information loop to connect with a school that is well suited to his or her talents? The Duke Ellington School of the Arts took that issue on directly by creating a "shepherding" program, in which twenty teachers serve as shepherds or mentors for incoming ninth- and tenth-graders. The individual attention helps students in both school and social life, easing the kids over the rough spots, and setting them up for success rather than failure.

CHAPTER 5

Leaders

My job is to find leaders for schools.

—John Murphy, Superintendent of Schools
Charlotte-Mecklenburg County, NC

Every successful Next Century School has at least one effective leader. In fact, strong leadership is the single feature that distinguishes the best Next Century Schools from others. In every school that has dramatically boosted student performance, changed the attitudes of students and teachers, or implemented radical reforms, there is a visionary and forceful individual leading the way.

Often the leaders of Next Century Schools are principals. However, leadership has also come from governors like Bill Clinton, Lamar Alexander, and Tom Kean. Sometimes it has emerged from education professionals: teachers, guidance counselors, or outsiders who may have a strong interest in education.

The importance of leadership in school reform will not surprise most people outside of public education. From Harvard Business School to the U.S. Army, the students of organizational success stress leadership. Entire industries exist to train leaders; organizations devote millions to their development; dozens of books are published annually that describe the techniques and secrets of leadership.

Leaders are especially critical to organizations that must adapt and change. Without a leader who can articulate a new mission, an organization will plow straight ahead, a creature of habit. Without a leader who can organize and motivate others to pursue a new strategy, an organization will follow its traditional modes of operation, or pursue the private agendas of its members or employees. Without leaders, organizations will do the same thing tomorrow that they did today.

Ironically, public schools, which need leaders who can promote change, have systematically restricted the power of principals and teachers to lead. Schools operate in a web of restrictions, from the federal government, which puts detailed prescriptions on how schools may use its money, to the states, whose bureaucracies define the schools' goals, curriculum, and textbooks. Often the greatest limits on leadership are imposed by local school district bureaucracies, whose supervisors, requisition forms, hiring rules, and the like can smother any local initiative before it begins. In many jurisdictions, rigid union relationships or inflexible contracts further constrain would-be school leaders.

More damaging than these barriers to leadership is the lack of systematic efforts by school systems to find and promote high-quality leaders. More than most other institutions, leaders of public schools are chosen on the basis of credentials and education, rather than demonstrated ability and performance. With few avenues for advancement, many ambitious teachers aspire to be principals. But access to this job is restricted by a web of rules and barriers. To be elevated to the principal's office, individuals must have passed through a thicket of education courses that have little to do with effective school management. Rare is the principal who is trained to get the highest performance from teachers and students. Virtually no school principals are recruited from outside the education community.

No other institution in society picks its leaders in this

Leaders

way. Credentials and education may be important, especially in technically oriented institutions, but leaders are selected because of their skills and abilities with people and process, not their résumés.

In a business setting, leadership is sometimes defined as the ability to motivate the members of a group to follow a course of action, usually without coercing them. As John Kotten of Harvard Business School notes, leaders must be able to:

- Devise and articulate a vision;

- Set a strategy for achieving it;

- Build a network of people who agree with and can help to accomplish the vision; and

- Motivate these people (and others outside the organization) to work hard to realize the vision.

Organizations that are consistently successful, on the battlefield or in the marketplace, pay careful attention to finding and nurturing people who can do these things. As Kotten notes, many attributes of a leader are important: analytic capacity, communication skills, experience, decisiveness, the ability to work through others, and high energy. At the Naval Academy and West Point, teaching young people these types of leadership skills is given top priority. Teaching leadership is considered more important than instruction in the techniques of battle, or the required courses in science and math. The importance attached to leadership is prompted not by military philosophy, but by the hard facts of military history: Successful armies and navies have always been led by great leaders, who may or may not have had detailed knowledge of military science and technique.

Similarly, at many companies that must respond constantly to rapidly changing environments, leadership is considered the key to sustained success. At Hewlett-Packard, for example, the job of recruiting the next generation of leaders is considered so important that it is a part of every manager's assignment, not just the responsibility of the human resources department. Leaders are shepherded by assigned mentors, and groomed with a structured series of responsibilities and specialized courses. These companies work hard to foster a culture that encourages and rewards people who show leadership.

Public schools, of course, are neither armies, where leaders can command, nor businesses, with the substantial incentives and resources to hire and motivate leaders. But schools setting out into new directions must still find leaders who can chart the new course, and who can get the crew to pull together.

Leadership Profiles

Who are these leaders in schools? Where do they come from? What do they do? How can school districts recruit and develop more leaders to leverage change and improve performance? The experience of successful Next Century Schools offers some insights.

Donna Hardy,
New Stanley Elementary

In February of 1990, David Lusk, the Superintendent of Schools for Kansas City, Kansas, arranged a meeting with the principal and teachers of one of the schools in his district, Stanley Elementary. Lusk's message was simple and breathtaking. He wanted their help in transforming Stanley from a struggling, unremarkable, inner-city school into a showcase of educational performance. He proposed that the school operate all year, using teams of teachers; that it recruit the diverse parents in its community to work in the school; that it abolish traditional grades in favor of mastery learning; and that it guarantee that *every* child graduating from the school would perform at or above grade level.

When he finished outlining his plans, he offered the teachers and the principal a choice. They could stay, knowing that the next several years would be a maelstrom of work, change, and emotional challenge. Or they could transfer to some other school in the district where the pressure would not be so great. In the end, only the principal, Donna Hardy, and five teachers stayed. For the opening of what was to be called "New" Stanley Elementary in September 1990, nine new teachers were recruited.

For Hardy, the challenge of transforming her school was terrifying, but irresistible. Over the next six months she and the teachers of New Stanley, along with planners from the district offices, worked long hours to prepare for the new program. Besides applying for and winning a grant to become a Next Century School, the team undertook a sweeping effort to educate themselves and their community about the coming changes. In particular, Hardy and her teachers devoted great time and energy to understanding and implementing the goal of mastery learning. The teachers agreed to set a target that any child leaving the school after at least four years of instruction at New Stanley would be at or above grade level. Although every teacher who had agreed to work at the school had verbally agreed with the idea that every child can learn, it turned out to be a staggering effort to define and then implement a program that would not allow any child to fail. In each subject teachers were asked to define specifically what constituted mastery of the subject, and what interim levels of achievement they would certify. Then they had to define the program of instruction, repetition, coaching, parental assistance, peer tutoring, or other strategies that could truly ensure that no child would fall below grade level.

Once the teachers were selected and the teams formed, they fanned out into the community to visit every parent. Consequently, a far broader parent volunteer organization was formed, and new roles for these volunteers were defined.

The building itself was revamped, not just with paint and physical improvement, but with computers.

Through this intensive effort, Donna Hardy was the hub of many wheels of activity. She selected teachers, organized teams, helped plan curriculum changes, worked with district planning staff, spoke to community groups, and listened patiently to the frustrations and doubts of her team. No one worked harder or longer. No one articulated the vision of what they were trying to achieve more often or more clearly than she.

Donna Hardy had plenty of help, both from her dedicated, self-selected teachers and, more importantly, from the superintendent's staff, who took a direct and personal interest in the success of the project. They always seemed to be able to find a way to acquire that extra item, to bend the rigid rule, or to cajole the balky bureaucrat who threatened success. In many ways, New Stanley was a test of their ideas in action, and they were intent upon success.

Although the results from the experiment are still coming in, the transformation at the school is already astounding. Student grades and test scores are up sharply. Attitude surveys among both teachers and students indicate a high level of satisfaction and enthusiasm. Even a casual visitor to the school feels a sense of accomplishment and excitement among most students and teachers.

Some five hundred visitors from other schools and communities have come to observe and ask questions about the school's formula for progress. Within the district, more than half a dozen other schools have decided to adopt New Stanley's approach.

New Stanley's most enthusiastic boosters are its parents. From a community that was detached and sometimes doubtful about the school and its programs, most parents have been transformed into supporters and participants. The principal regularly receives calls from parents whose only complaint is that some families with children out of the district are lying about their addresses to enroll their children at New Stanley. The school's reputation has improved so dramatically that real estate agents have found that an address within New Stanley's boundaries helps to sell or rent property, despite the rundown condition of many of the houses in the neighborhood.

Before the school district officials gave Donna Hardy the power and the resources to chart her own course, she had simply been one among many principals in the district struggling to improve the performance of her school. But once she and her team chose to accept the freedom they were offered, she became a visible standout as a school leader. Although the specific reforms undertaken at New Stanley are important, even more important is the way in which Donna Hardy has led her team to implement radical change in the school.

Norm Higgins, Piscataquis Community High

Norm Higgins had already been the principal of Piscataquis Community High School in Guilford, Maine, for eight years when he decided to apply for a grant from the Next Century Schools program in 1990. It was Higgins's first attempt to win major outside funding, and he believed that his school was ready to undertake the bold reforms envisioned by the RJR Nabisco Foundation.

Piscataquis Community High School is a small school at the center of a rural community that stretches across an area the size of Rhode Island in northwestern Maine. Even before Higgins and his small cadre of teachers decided to undertake a reform program at Piscataquis, the newly installed superintedent, Ray Poulin, Jr., had been encouraging schools across the district to strike out in new directions. Since arriving in 1987, Poulin had delegated substantial budgetary, hiring, and other decision-making authority to school principals. For Higgins, the freedom he had, combined with the money from the Foundation, was an extraordinary opportunity.

In defining his vision for the school, Higgins set some simple, yet high goals. Although Piscataquis historically had sent a lower proportion of its graduates on to college compared to other high schools in Maine, Higgins promised that 80 percent of his students would go on to institutions of higher education.

And despite the presence of many low-performing students, the school decided to institute a difficult, locally developed competency test, and to have 90 percent of all students master it.

Early in the process of defining his vision for the school, Higgins began to search for help from the leaders among his teachers, by sharing his ideas, but listening as well. To accomplish these goals, Higgins established a leadership committee composed of teachers from the school. At several staff retreats designed to define and develop the changes in the school program, this leadership group forged a bond of teamwork that gradually took ownership of the reform program away from the principal. "I learned," says Higgins, "that teachers can do it better; that teachers can do it faster; and that teachers rewrote my job description."

Assistance from outside the school also played a part. Two consultants from the University of Maine, Dick Babb and Russ Quaglia, helped teachers understand, engineer, and grow with the changes in the school. The supportive school board that trusted the teachers and principal enough to allow them to experiment also made a positive difference.

In one important respect, Piscataquis is like many rural and even semi-urban schools outside the nation's fast-growing cities and suburbs: Demographic change is slow. Many Piscataquis students are the sons and daughters of Piscataquis graduates (and drop-outs), and the teachers not only know younger brothers and sisters, but parents, aunts and uncles, and cousins. This means that many of the adults who earned GEDs at Piscataquis were once full-time students there—until they dropped out.

But the most important aspect of the Piscataquis experience is the transformation of the teaching force from conventional men and women to extraordinary men and women. A towering example is Donna Vigure, a teacher of English literature, who was convinced that only the best and the brightest could deal with a demanding curriculum. She only taught Dostoyevsky to her most promising seniors, and when principal Norm Higgins asked her to enlarge the class she resisted—heroically. She was convinced that regular kids weren't up to the demands of *The Possessed* or *The Brothers K.* Norm Higgins convinced her she was wrong. And now that she is teaching everyone her demanding course, her students—and visitors—are convinced that she is doing something right. Donna's Dostoyevsky seminar, for about twenty upperclassmen (and women) is a wonder to behold. Meeting for two periods (part of Piscataquis's block scheduling), she runs the class like an Oxford seminar. The Socratic method is the approach, and the students are prepared—they've read the text and are ready for tough, probing, and sensitive questions. As a consequence, they provide tough, probing, and sensitive answers. The seminar, made up of ordinary kids, achieves extraordinary results because by expecting much of her students they expect much of themselves. Donna's high school seminar would grace any Ivy League College.

This pit-bull approach to mastery by every child is having its effect. At the end of the 1992 school year, some 70 percent of graduating seniors were headed off to higher education, up 20 percentage points from the year before. Higgins, however, asserts that the most exciting results will show up in the years ahead. "We will do even better than we hoped," he says.

When Piscataquis won the Next Century Schools grant, Higgins was already a strong leader of his school. But the grant gave him the leverage he needed to take his vision for the school and make it happen.

126

Steve Ketcham,
University Terrace Elementary School

Steve Ketcham had been principal of University Terrace Elementary School for just over two years when a friend called to tell him about a press report describing the Next Century Schools program. For Ketcham, it was an opportunity that couldn't be missed. "We had to improve things dramatically here," he said. "The only alternative was to close the school."

Although University Terrace is only blocks from the campus of Louisiana's State University in East Baton Rouge, its students' lives are remote from the opportunities of higher education. More than 90 percent of the students are from minority backgrounds, and most are from poor families. Academic performance has traditionally lagged far behind other schools in the city and state.

But Ketcham saw opportunities for the students at University Terrace, while others saw overwhelming risks of failure. Immediately after learning of the grant announcement, Ketcham began assembling a small group of dedicated teachers to define their plans for reforming the school. Urged on by personnel from the school district, there soon were teams of teachers and other school personnel fleshing out programs. The school proposed to shift its structure entirely away from traditional grade/age groupings to multi-age/achievement-level classes. Instruction was individualized with personal education plans. Parents were enlisted to become advocates for students without parental support. A longer school day and school year were proposed. Computerized instruction was brought into the school.

Ketcham was convinced that "summer learning loss" was a serious problem. Most of his students came from impoverished backgrounds, and they quickly lagged behind their more affluent contemporaries. The solution? More "time on task," the one thing that education research is unequivocal about. Kids learn what they study; the more they study, the more they are likely to learn. All things being equal, more is better; "good" time on task is better yet. Combine quality time and quantity and you have a winner.

When the school's application to the Foundation won a grant, Ketcham's irrepressible enthusiasm began to leverage a genuine rebirth of education quality at the school. With project manager Mauritta Hurst providing organizational and planning support, the team began to win converts among teachers and students. Despite the overwhelming problems faced by many families, increasing numbers of parents in the community began to share the beliefs of the school leaders that University Terrace children could indeed overcome the obstacles they faced.

Two years later, officials from the district, parents, and long-time teachers in the school marvel at the transformation under way at University Terrace. The physical appearance of the school has been enhanced with shrubbery, carpentry projects, and paint. Veteran teachers report that they have fallen in love with their profession again. Student scores and attitudes have risen dramatically. Far from closing University Terrace, the district is exploring plans to emulate its approach across the district. Virtually everyone connected with the school cites Steve Ketcham as the "Pied Piper" who led this parade toward success.

At University Terrace, Ketcham led the school in new directions, from what seemed like a blind alley with no exits. Yet his tenacious and inspirational vision, coupled with outside assistance, started a process that is dramatically improving the school and even the community's belief in itself and its children.

Lessons of Leadership

These and similar stories of leadership and change could be repeated in different ways at each of the most successful Next Century Schools. The stories reveal a remarkably consistent pattern, and illustrate lessons for other communities seeking to create outstanding schools. Six lessons stand out:

1. SUPPORT FROM OUTSIDE THE SCHOOL IS ESSENTIAL.

Allowing leaders to emerge in schools that have typically suppressed leadership usually requires action from people outside the school. At New Stanley, district planners and leaders actively sought out the school as a candidate for reform, delegated power to the school's principal to pursue change, and encouraged her to strike out on her own. Without this empowerment, Donna Hardy and her team could never have undertaken or accomplished so much. At Piscataquis and University Terrace, the spark came from within the school, but outside administrators provided active support, and great freedom for the principals to act.

In some cases, outside support and pressure can even stimulate individuals to accept leadership roles despite their own personal reluctance. At Douglas Byrd Junior High School, Principal Larry Lancaster grudgingly allowed Rosie Bullard, one of his eager staff members, to propose a sweeping reform of educational practices in the school. A self-described autocrat in management style, Lancaster was stunned when the proposal was funded. "I was naive" about what was entailed in the plan, he now says. "I didn't know all this would happen." With encouragement and pressure from the new district superintendent, and enthusiastic energy from some of his staff, Lancaster undertook the sweeping changes. Now, two years later, the project has changed Lancaster as much as it has changed the school. Teachers and students praise his new flexibility and willingness to implement changes. "I wasn't even scratching the surface," he says about his previous approach to management. "But I said I was going to do it, and I've had to do it."

In some ways, the process of applying for and winning a grant provided important, outside support for school leaders. Many principals found that their independence and credibility within the school community was tremendously strengthened when they won a grant, which supplied significant levels of funding from outside the district flowing directly to the school. On the other hand, resistance from school-district officials can sometimes squelch the plans of even the most dedicated and resourceful leaders. At Nathan Hale Junior High School in Brooklyn, New York, Principal Charles Dluzniewski had to spend months cajoling the district administrators to allow him access to the money the school had won. Energy that should have gone toward exciting teachers and parents was directed at devising clever ways around the byzantine New York City requisition process. Although Nathan Hale has made progress toward improving its school environment, the results have been slow and uneven compared to the needs of the school and its students.

2. THE MOST IMPORTANT LEADERSHIP STEP IS BUILDING A TEAM.

The school leaders who were the most able to generate change did so by inspiring those around them to share their ideas. Hardy, Higgins, and Ketcham developed their ideas with the help of leadership teams of co-workers, with whom they shared the responsibility and credit. The leaders sought to infect others with their own enthusiasm for the opportunities, and to create a ripple of excitement that would gradually spread. For Donna Hardy, the task of finding these disciples was simplified by the departure of teachers who did not want to go forward, and their replacement with newly hired supporters. For Higgins and Ketcham, the task was to find allies within the ranks of their best professionals and to use these to leverage more change among others who initially were skeptical.

In every case, these leaders gave up considerable power to their co-workers on leadership teams. At New Stanley, teachers set their own agendas for training, curriculum development, and mastery learning. Hardy did not impose her judgement, but did more listening than talking. At Piscataquis, Norm Higgins found that his ideas improved when they were reinvented by his teachers.

On the other hand, would-be leaders who could not share their vision, delegate responsibility, or cede control soon found themselves isolated and unable to progress. One small, rural school in the Pine Barrens of New Jersey reached the finals of the two-stage award process only to drop out because the school principal failed to inform the school board about his intentions. The announcement that the school had advanced to the finals came as a complete surprise to the board. But the New Jersey Pine Barrens school was not alone; a brilliant and exciting proposal from a school on the Flat Head Reservation near Glacier National Park in Montana met the same fate. And an equally interesting proposal from a suburban Pennsylvania district failed to attract the support of the school's teachers and parents. Apparently working in semi-isolation, an inventive and imaginative principal had failed to involve his community—to his chagrin. They turned on the proposal, and launched a letter-writing campaign to the Foundation asking that the proposal *not* be funded. Truth is stranger than fiction!

Is there a lesson in this? We think so. These misadventures should remind us all that school reform is risky business, hard to conceptualize, harder to do. In several cases, schools presented exciting proposals in the first round of the selection process, but were unable to reach agreement on a final submission. Each time the explanation was that no strong, cohesive team had been formed to develop the ideas and plans contained in the original submission. Leaders must inspire followers.

3. SUCCESSFUL LEADERS ARE GOOD COMMUNICATORS AND MARKETERS.

A key part of the task of building a team is constant communication. The best school leaders are those who are constantly repeating and reinvigorating their vision of success in front of many audiences. Steve Ketcham is a tireless proponent of his vision, before community groups, parents, district officials, teachers, and students. In fact, virtually every Next Century School leader has reported that the time and resources allocated to communication with the various constituencies is far greater than they had imagined.

But this constant communication pays off. In Mooresville, North Carolina, Superintendent Sam Houston and Principal Carol Carroll decided that year-round schooling was critical to the success of many of their disadvantaged students. Together they spent months convincing the school board and the community to allow a voluntary year-round school plan to go into effect, and to get teachers and parents to agree that it would not disrupt lives built around the traditional nine-month school year. But once they were allowed to implement the plan, it caught fire. "I would never go back to the old system," says one teacher in a typical comment. The voluntary program has become virtually universal, and other schools in the district and the state have decided to implement a similar system. Communication pays.

4. MANY CONTRIBUTE, THE PRINCIPAL LEADS.

Without a competent, caring, communicative, and high-energy person in the principal's position, the task of school reform is very difficult. Reform can be initiated from outside the school or stimulated from within. But in the end, it is the principal who implements and sustains the changes through the inevitable roller-coaster of euphoria and setbacks. Among Next Century Schools there is an almost perfect correlation between the strength and skills of the principal and the performance of the school. Increasingly, picking winning schools has been a matter of picking winning principals.

The ideal principal has the confidence to delegate substantial amounts of power to teachers, and to demand accountability from them. He or she is likely to be good at selling ideas, and to be willing to work tirelessly to accomplish major goals. Good principals are likely to be able to devise a strategy for working with, around, or through any individual or group.

5. LEADERS PERFORM BEST WHEN THEY ARE IN CHARGE, AND ARE HELD ACCOUNTABLE FOR STUDENT PERFORMANCE.

The RJR Nabisco Foundation offered significant amounts of money to individual schools. In many cases this money, coupled with administrative flexibility, allowed schools to hire additional staff people of their own choosing. The Foundation required that every school present a plan for measuring its own performance, including targets they expected to achieve.

While this responsibility seems routine to most executives, it was viewed as a revolution in many schools. Many had no procedures for handling money, setting budget priorities, or tracking expenditures against targets. Many were unfamiliar with how to develop plans for measuring the results of their financial and human investments. And for most, the opportunity to hire staff directly was an unfamiliar process.

Previously, of course, these responsibilities were handled almost entirely at the district level. While most principals certainly exert some control over hiring in their schools, they have little flexibility to set spending priorities or reassign responsibilities among staff. Although they must administer a continuous battery of standardized tests, most principals have no idea of how to measure their own performance or that of students and teachers, or to calibrate these results against goals or spending.

However, in each of the Next Century Schools, the process of controlling spending and measuring results has changed the attitudes and the approach of principals. They have found that the tools and the discipline of combining authority and responsibility have significantly changed how they operate. For example, many schools entering their second and third years as Next Century Schools have made major shifts in personnel, or in the direction of their programs. Some of these changes have been the result of systematic measurement or reviews, but more often they have simply resulted from careful reassessment of what is required to expand the success of the program. In all cases, however, it is the responsibility for results that has made school leaders more concerned with the performance of their teachers and students, and more willing to push for change. Rather than accept mediocre performance, school principals who face scrutiny concerning the overall school results are pushing for results from students and from the teachers who work with them.

6. TEACHER LEADERS ARE CRUCIAL TO SCHOOL SUCCESS.

Most schools have a few teachers whose skills and approach are respected and imitated by others. These talented individuals seldom directly supervise or train other teachers, but their professionalism is often transmitted to others in the school on a gradual and voluntary basis.

Among Next Century Schools, these teacher leaders have achieved much greater influence and impact. When new challenges are placed before the entire teaching staff as part of goal-setting or implementing new ideas, it is the lead teachers whose opinions, approach, and style are often followed. These teachers, who might previously have been merely examples of good practice within the school, become more actively sought out by others. Their philosophies and techniques become the benchmarks for performance in the school; often their specific teaching methods are adopted by others. And because they often undertake direct leadership roles in team-teaching situations or as leaders of committees, their influence is further extended.

As one school visitor noted, the most telling reflection of the new power of teacher leaders was reflected in the teacher lounge. "At Union House," he reported, "the teachers don't lounge. They plan programs and strategies, they discuss and critique innovative approaches, and they share problem-solving ideas, including offering assistance even if they are not charged with the responsibility." The school has become a place where the best teachers have been empowered to be leaders.

Tasks for School Communities Who Want Change

These lessons from Next Century Schools have obvious implications for other schools that intend to significantly change their programs or improve their results. They suggest that superintendents, parents, or community leaders working with schools should be concerned first with the quality of the leaders in their schools. To do this, school communities must take three steps.

1. CHOOSE PRINCIPALS WHO CAN LEAD.

The principal is the individual with the greatest influence over the success of any school. The primary task of superintendents, or others with an impact on the selection of school principals, should be to find leaders: Individuals who can communicate, who have earned the respect of teachers, students, and parents, who have energy and enthusiasm, who can inspire teams of professionals, and who can understand school problems and develop sound strategies to deal with them.

Such individuals may not come exclusively from the ranks of the teaching staff, nor even from the school system itself. In the same way that talented managers and leaders in business may be able to shift successfully from one industry to another, or from the profit-making to the nonprofit world, great leaders of schools may come from entirely outside the system in some cases. The majority, however, will be promoted from the professional teaching ranks. Every effort should be made to seek out and groom talented teachers for leadership roles. In the same way that change-oriented businesses develop programs that recruit or identify high-potential individuals and systematically prepare them for later leadership roles, school systems should develop programs that look for and develop leaders.

There is no limit to the "principle" that the principal is all-important, whether the school is relatively advantaged, as is Bloomfield Hills, or impoverished, as is Snively Elementary. Home to countless migrant families over the years, Snively begins to lose its children in late April as fruit-picking in the North begins. The principal and her staff were convinced that extending the school year was critically important to Snively's population, and they have convinced their students of this as well. When a newspaper reporter visited Snively in early June—when the rest of the students in the country were out for the summer—she asked some sixth-graders why they were still in school. Maria, one sixth-grader, responded: "I need more time in school so I can be a better student in seventh grade. I'm glad to be here because there isn't much to do at home and going to school

here is fun. It's a lot better than picking fruit in the groves."
An inspired principal, with a supportive staff, can even swim
against the tide of custom and children's strong reluctance
to attend school in summer.

2. GIVE SCHOOL LEADERS FREEDOM AND CONTROL.

Unless leaders are given the power to perform, they cannot. The simple step of giving leaders control causes
changes that promote the kind of performance parents and
the community hope for.

One of the most striking lessons of Next Century
Schools was the way leaders emerged in response to the opportunity to change the school. Given the freedom to manage their own budgets and the task of defining their own
goals, most schools found individuals within the school who
could realize the school's vision. This freedom for leaders to
emerge is missing in large school bureaucracies. Surrounded by specifications for textbooks, requirements for
what, when, how, and how much to teach, and rules and regulations governing virtually every kind of activity, schools
are trapped in red tape.

Good people must have the authority and responsibility
to do their jobs at the individual school-building level. Because schools should be held accountable for performance,
virtually every decision about how to educate children
should be made by the responsible teachers and staff. Hiring, firing, and most budget decisions should be made at the
school level. How, when, and what to teach should be decided primarily by teachers.

3. SET STANDARDS, AND INSIST THAT PERFORMANCE BE MEASURED.

This freedom for school leaders to act carries with it the responsibility to produce results. Those in the wider community outside the school—such as parents, businesspeople, district officials, and taxpayers—must insist that schools provide them with detailed evidence concerning the academic performance of their students, and the satisfaction of parents, employees, and students. Those outside the school should support its independence, encourage its change process, and demand that it produce.

The Key to Successful Change: Communication

Success is most likely to be developed when large numbers of teachers, parents, children, and community leaders share a vision for how a school should perform. Leaders have the primary responsibility for opening up the channels of communication that lead to such a shared vision. Not only should principals be the chief marketers of their schools, they should be willing to operate in a highly interactive environment of sharing ideas, and sharing power with teachers, parents, and even students.

School communication is more than a matter of public relations, it means communicating substance—what the school's purposes are, and what its serious activities are. This applies not just to the school as it relates to the larger world beyond its doors, but within the school as well. One of the most important tasks of school leaders is to let students know what is expected of them, the consequences of failure, and rewards of success. In addition, school leaders must in-

139

form employees what is expected of them and how they can improve.

No task is more important for public schools than that of developing their leadership. The Next Century Schools program has proven that there are leaders in many schools. If America has great public schools in the next century, it will largely be because, school by school and community by community, the public school system has found leaders, given them the tools to do the job, set standards for performance, and then gotten out of the way.

CHAPTER 6

Teachers: Developing a School's Human Capital

We realized that if anything is going to happen, teachers have to make it happen.

—Sandy Lenning, Teacher at Denali Elementary
Fairbanks, Alaska

When Chelsea High School opened, every Friday afternoon June Murray, Mary Driscoll, and Frank DeVito would row across the Boston Harbor with their students. Before they joined the staff at Chelsea, none of the three had ever handled an oar in a racing shell. With help from the Hull Life Saving Museum, they learned the skills and teamwork of competitive rowing along with their students.

These are not typical field trips with structured learning objectives, or classroom exercises to be integrated into Monday's lessons. They are simply physical learning experiences in which the teachers in Chelsea's Next Century School Pathways program participate. "We're trying to break down the traditional student-staff barriers by giving students a chance to see us as learners, like them," says Maggie Lodge, the program coordinator at Chelsea. "This hadn't always been easy, not only physically but emotionally. No one likes to look incompetent in front of others, but when you're learning, it's inevitable. But it's a great way to build our relationships with the students."

The Pathways program at Chelsea is unusual in many ways because it serves school drop-outs during nontradi-

143

tional afternoon hours. But in some ways Chelsea is typical of the extraordinary changes taking place in the roles of teachers at many Next Century Schools. Far from the stand-up-and-lecture-the-class traditions of school teaching, NCS teachers are experimenting with radical changes in every aspect of their jobs.

Of course, virtually every public school can boast of a few excellent, innovative teachers. And most people can remember great teachers from their own years in school— caring adults who excited youthful imaginations, or inspired hard work and achievement. The new roles being undertaken by teachers in Next Century Schools extend beyond isolated classrooms, however well-taught, to include basic changes that affect the entire staffs of many schools. More than islands of excellence, NCS schools are systematically changing the strategies and approaches of virtually all teachers: redefining the job of teaching itself.

Although there is no single formula or model that describes the new roles of teachers in Next Century Schools, one theme describes many of the shifts: *changing relationships*. Teachers are transforming their relationships with each other, with their students, with technology and tools, with their careers, and with their unions and managers. Rather than remaining in their traditional position, isolated from each other and from the community outside the school, teachers are becoming more integrated into teams and networks that extend beyond the classroom. And more than simply lecturing to twenty-five or thirty students for fifty minutes at a time, teachers are establishing ties with students that reach outside the classroom and extend over many years.

Along with these new relationships has come a new sense of professionalism. Like doctors or engineers, teachers are taking responsibility for the development of their own skills. They are more conscious of the need to satisfy their clients, and they are more likely to think of themselves as managers of people, tools, and technologies, rather than as workers on a line, assembling children. Simply put, NCS teachers are redefining their organizations and rewriting the rules of their profession.

Redefinition is essential for many reasons, not least the continuing danger of teacher burnout. The stress of teaching, particularly in a bureaucratic environment, is hard to overestimate. True, many jobs are extremely stressful, from cops on the mean streets to scrub nurses in the emergency room, but the solution is often the same: Give the individual maximum professional running room and the stress is more effectively managed. In case after case, Next Century Schools teachers report that their new professional responsibilities—and opportunities—have kept them in the profession. Half the teachers at Park View Elementary School in Mooresville, North Carolina, for example, had been planning to retire or find other employment. Their experiment with year-round schools rekindled the spark, and they remained with the program. But is this a one-time shot? Teachers report that it isn't, that the new format is what makes the difference. The ability to bring children along successfully, by assigning slow kids to intersession remedial work and fast kids to intersession enrichment programs, means that kids are neither frustrated nor bored when they return to the regular program. Teachers also enjoy high self-esteem because they are successful.

Similarly, teachers in the Marshall Early Learning Center in Marshall, Wisconsin, report that the opportunity to draw upon the community—to pull parents into the program—has made a major difference to them. Teachers need a sense of efficacy, a sense that what they are doing is worthwhile and that it works, just as the rest of us do. Dwight Morrow High School in Englewood, New Jersey, offers a dramatic case in point. Coordinator Jay Shapiro was looking forward to early retirement and beginning a new career in real estate. As his fifty-fifth birthday approached Jay was encouraged by his principal to attend afternoon workshops and teach summer school in preparation for a major restructuring effort. He became totally absorbed in the undertaking, developing an approach to dealing with his kids they'd never heard of before. He denied them "the right to fail"; it was a cop-out. If a student couldn't do it right the first time, second time, or third time, he or she had to come back for more. His students were energized, and Jay was too. He couldn't fail either; not only did he stay with teaching, but he has become the head of the Dwight Morrow's Next Century Schools program.

Teachers' New Roles

Inside Next Century Schools there are many versions of teachers' new roles. The most important are:

1. TEACHERS AS COACHES.

In the traditional school, teachers do the work. They plan lessons, make assignments, deliver lectures, interrogate students, and administer tests. The classic teacher instructs students. Nearly a decade ago, however, Mortimer Adler articulated a different vision of teaching in his book *The Paideia Proposal.* One of his fundamental insights was that the ideal teacher functions best as a coach of students, rather than as a master or instructor.

Teachers, Adler believes, must abandon their self-image as the suppliers of information, pouring knowledge into the empty heads of students assigned to them. Rather, the teacher must assist and coach students, helping them find their own path to knowledge and understanding. To Adler, the best teachers inspire and enable students to learn. Students are the workers, and the job of the teacher is to help them learn. Just as a coach assists his players on the field during a game, the teacher must also assist students in the game of learning. Teachers as coaches can ensure that students have learning tools; they can make knowledge readily available; they can motivate them to work hard; they can encourage them to work together to achieve joint objectives; and they can help students to value learning and respect knowledge. But teachers cannot simply coerce students to study, or command them to learn.

Teacher-coaches are similar in many ways to leaders operating in other environments. Just as a leader strives to define a vision and to mold a group into a team striving to achieve it, a teacher-coach must also seek to inspire students to set goals and take action to realize their goals. Like other leaders, teacher-coaches accomplish most when they motivate others to act, rather than directly through their own actions or orders.

Many Next Century Schools have been inspired by this vision of the teacher as a coach. Among them, few have succeeded as well as Piscataquis High School. At Piscataquis, many teachers have radically changed their approach to instruction. Following intensive training sessions and internal debates, teachers have begun to transform the process of learning in their classrooms.

Jim Drinkwater's sophomore American history classroom is a typical example. After students plow through material on the industrial revolution in America, filled with dates and inventions (Cyrus McCormick: the mechanical reaper, 1831; Robert Fulton: steamboat, 1807), Drinkwater stops the class to ask, "What does this era say about America today?" After a few tentative replies the class becomes alive. America, says one student, was taking inventions pioneered in Britain and Scotland, perfecting them, and applying them here. That's what Japan is doing to us today, says another. Soon the class is engaged in a debate over strategies for solving American industrial problems. For Drinkwater, the goal of teaching history has changed. Instead of demanding that his students master historical facts, he has enabled them to become excited about the meaning of history and its relevance to the present. "They may not remember exactly what year Fulton took his steamboat up the Hudson River, but I hope they'll understand better why it mattered then, and what it means today," he says.

Across Piscataquis and in many other Next Century Schools, the same scenes play out. In Socratic fashion, teachers are asking their students hard-to-answer questions, to which the answers are not always found in the book. Students are taking responsibility for their own learning; teachers have become coaches.

2. TEACHERS AS COUNSELORS.

Teachers cannot expect to inspire or lead students from a distance. The few feet between the desk at the front of the classroom and the rows of student desks often represents a wide psychological barrier separating teachers from children. Many Next Century Schools have recognized that this barrier must be breached if teachers are to motivate students to study and learn.

Again, there are always a few teachers whose personalities and style invite respect and friendship from students. But in many schools, even when teachers and students want to establish stronger relationships, the traditions and the structure of learning prevents much interaction. In particular, large schools that are organized into seven-period days virtually prohibit teachers or students from knowing each other well. A teacher who must instruct 125 children each day, 50 minutes at a time, in groups of 25, has little chance to spend more than a few minutes with each child. In a large high school with many teachers specializing in one subject at one grade level, teachers may be expected to relate to hundreds of children over the course of a single student's three- or four-year school career. Only a few lucky students can expect to know a teacher well under such circumstances.

In various ways many Next Century Schools have sought to rebuild relationships between students and teachers. One of the most frequent approaches is the "school-within-a-school." By creating smaller units focused on specific curricula, and organized around a smaller cadre of teachers, schools-within-schools help to create an environment that breaks down the anonymity in school and builds durable relationships between students and teachers.

Another approach is to keep the same teachers with children for several years to establish stronger, more stable adult-child relationships. Alternatively, some schools keep the same teachers with children for longer blocks of time through the school day.

All of these approaches are visible at Douglas Byrd Junior High in Fayetteville, North Carolina. At Byrd, incoming students who are at greater risk of dropping out of school are asked to join the STAR (Students and Teachers Achieving Results) program. STAR is an integrated program that unites forty students and their parents with two teachers. Rather than the students being shuffled off to classes throughout the school, the group remains together during the school day and stays with one or both of the same teachers for two years. The goal of the small classes and sustained relationships is to develop a rapport between the adults in the school and the children and their parents.

The initial results of the effort are striking: Among STAR students, there are fewer absences, fewer drop-outs, and higher scholastic achievement than among the rest of the student body. Many STAR parents who had once been unengaged with the school or their children's education have become actively involved. "It was the first time I had ever been called by someone from the school to tell me my child had done something good," remarked one parent.

Changing the structure of schooling is only one way to build new relationships between students and teachers. The goal of transforming the teacher into a counselor or advisor to students is explicitly made a part of the responsibilities of teachers at the Pathways program at Chelsea High School. Not only do teachers learn with students in the rowing program and other outdoor activities, but teachers have accepted the role of student advisor. Working entirely with students who have been overwhelmed by problems such as drug abuse, poverty, or teen pregnancies, Pathways teacher-advisors provide individualized attention to each child based on his or her needs. With small-group classes that run from 2:30 to 9 p.m. (to allow students to work in the mornings), Pathways strives to create an atmosphere of closeness among students and teachers. Each night, students and teachers eat dinner together, at a "family" meal they prepare.

Along with the mentors assigned to each child, teacher-advisors take personal responsibility for the progress of their students.

Maggie Lodge, the program coordinator, writes,

> The adoption of a teacher/advisor has allowed us to break down some of the barriers between staff and students which exist in a more traditional school setting. Each staff member has responsibility for a group of Pathway students. In advisory groups, teachers assist students with goal-setting, and provide additional academic and emotional support. In addition, teacher/advisors serve as liaisons between students' significant adults and the school.

The skills and backgrounds of the teacher-advisors reflect this emphasis on personal relationships with students. Several instructors came from counseling to their jobs. One is a graduate of the "streets" from where many of the students come. George Roman has a special respect from and empathy with the students because he was a school drop-out for years before returning to Chelsea to graduate recently.

Pathways' intensive emphasis on building relationships between adults and disadvantaged young people is expensive and difficult. In order to provide individualized attention and special small-group activities, a ratio of one adult to six children has been maintained. But to the leaders of the troubled Chelsea school system, the high price of reclaiming these troubled young people seems justified. Despite a year of severe budget cuts, including teacher layoffs and firings, the Pathways program has survived. To the new leaders of the public school system, the chance to prove that a public school program can finally succeed with young people who have always failed in school is too important to be compromised.

3. TEACHERS AS LEARNING MANAGERS.

Many teachers in public schools feel like cogs in a big machine. They are assigned rooms, children, hours, subjects, and course materials. After a specified period, the children are expected to leave the rooms carrying some part of the course materials in their heads. Although this highly structured environment is comforting and familiar to both students and teachers, it does not always work well in promoting curiosity or understanding. Often teachers may feel they lack the time or the freedom to direct each student's learning, or to manage individual instruction.

The Recess Math program at Davis Elementary School in Portland, Oregon, turns these traditional structures upside down. Although the program has a room, every other aspect of the children's exploration of mathematics is selected and managed by the teachers. The objective is simple: to stimulate curiosity about and understanding of mathematical concepts. Beginning first as a collection of math materials, and later expanded to include computers, games, puzzles, books, and other materials, the program had evolved into a constantly changing array of mathematics-related activities that supplement the work done in regular classroom settings. Because recess and after-school periods are often short, and children of different ages and abilities are moving in and out of the math lab at various times, the teachers must manage the instructional activities of many individuals and groups simultaneously.

Yet, in the hands of skillful and enthusiastic teachers, Recess Math works. As one observer commented:

Children look forward to coming to the Recess Math. They come on their own, unaccompanied by adults, often after completing a quick lunch. Most of the older children move directly to the computers, while the young children move to the games or blocks or other activities that excite them. Once the children have arrived, learning activities commence with the teacher and her assistants working with the children in groups, and at times, as a whole class. There are no apparent discipline problems. This is not a helter-skelter atmosphere with children moving from one spot to another, having little sense of direction. Rather, these children are guided skillfully by the staff and are working continuously with math concepts in a variety of ways.

Christine Anderson, the teacher who managed this program during its first year, found her role to be much different than her role in the classroom she left. Far more than in her well-organized class, she was forced to be a coordinator and manager of tools (computers, math manipulatives, and games) and people (students and teaching assistants). Although she succeeded brilliantly in the first year (school-wide math scores climbed much faster than those of similar students elsewhere in the district), the experience was challenging and stressful. Donnise Brown, principal at Davis and an architect of Recess Math, observed that Recess Math may require a different kind of teacher. "Most teachers need the relative safety and comfort of their four walls. Programs like this, where you have to be constantly adapting to changing learning situations, demand a different set of skills and attitudes. Many teachers still prefer the traditional setting."

In schools that are beginning to use technology and new

learning techniques for instruction, however, the traditional setting is changing. Instead of a single teacher instructing all children in the same thing at the same time, students are engaging in a variety of activities at once. Some may work with different software; some may be engaged in cooperative groups; and some may be with tutors. In such settings, the teacher must coordinate the work, meshing people, learning aids, and students into productive combinations. This new role is more complicated and creative, and it demands more managerial skills. But the result of teachers becoming learning managers is typically better student performance.

4. TEACHERS AS PARTICIPANTS.

"Teaching," says Al Shanker, "is a lonely profession." Although school hallways and cafeterias are teeming with children, and most schools have at least a dozen adults on the staff, most teachers spend their days in the relative isolation of their classrooms. Unlike other professionals, who are routinely connected to colleagues and contemporaries by a web of telephones, faxes, and meetings, teachers are cut off from each other. Typically, a few telephone lines are shared by an entire school. Teachers find time to talk to one another over hurried lunches or at weekly staff meetings, while interaction with parents is channeled into monthly PTA meetings.

Managers from other industries, especially those that provide information services, would be surprised by the isolation of employees in schools. In the modern economy, the exchange of information among workers and others is the key to performance and productivity (although office workers never tire of complaining about how unproductive their endless meetings and phone calls are). The process of information exchange—the endless networking of people and

154

ideas—is expensive and time-consuming. But it is indispensable, whether the product is office equipment, automobiles, health care, or hotel rooms.

But in schools, whose business is the distribution of information, teachers are islands. With few tools to encourage interaction, and little time built into the school day for information exchanges, teachers find that they are working together only in the strictly physical sense of being in the same building. Once classes start, teachers are on their own.

One hallmark of Next Century Schools has been an attempt to break down the isolation. Many of the programs that won grants involved additional time away from the classroom for teachers to plan, exchange information, and learn from each other. Particularly in schools that were embarking on major departures from traditional programs, planning time was essential, both in the summers and during the school year. At Piscataquis, the entire teaching staff spent several summer days together at a team-building retreat in the mountains; in the fall these team-building exercises continued with help from outside facilitators. At other successful Next Century Schools like New Stanley in Kansas, or Linda Vista in California, the time allocated to planning increased significantly, both during paid working hours, and on a volunteer basis after school.

Many schools also restructured classroom assignments to create teams of teachers. Of course, team teaching has been used in some public schools for decades, to help teachers manage schedules, increase planning time, and add new skills to classrooms. But at some Next Century Schools, team teaching has become the vehicle for changing the way teachers relate to each other and to their students. At Franklin Junior High in Brainerd, Minnesota, for example, team teaching is a central feature of the school's reforms. During the first year of the grant, two pilot groups of four teachers were organized, with each group sharing responsibility for 125 students. Teachers met daily to plan interdisciplinary units that link content and instructional strategies, to discuss specific students, or to resolve problems. At a typical meeting, one teacher reported on a training seminar covering "Outcomes Based Education"; the discussion moved to plans for a coming field trip and a conference that requested a speaker from the school; later three of the teachers developed a coordinated plan to deal with one young man who seemed to be falling behind his classmates.

The discussion of the failing student illustrates a new sense of shared responsibility among team members. To some degree, every team member feels he or she has a stake in the success of every other teacher in the group and for every child in the group. At Franklin, which is trying to implement the philosophy that no child can fail, the performance of every student in the group reflects on all of the teachers. Just as peer pressure among students can be harnessed to lift weaker students to perform better, so support and attention from peers can encourage innovation and improvement among teachers. "Team teaching has brought back a sense of community among our kids and us," said one team member. "They know four teachers care about them."

Some of the team teachers were initially skeptical of the teaming idea, preferring their old classroom routines. But the experience has won enthusiastic praise from virtually every team member. "Issues that used to fester for weeks or months can be hashed out in a few minutes now," commented one teacher. "The barriers between teachers and teachers, and teachers and students are being broken down," says another. "I don't feel isolated anymore. . . . I can see real connections," observed one veteran math teacher, who had almost decided to leave teaching, but has decided to stay with the profession.

The early experiments with team teaching at Franklin have now won many new converts. The early results for students were positive, with fewer low grades and lower drop-out rates. During the second year of the program, virtually every teacher opted to join a team, and the concept has been adopted throughout the school.

5. TEACHERS AS LEADERS.

Just as the traditional organization of the school has tended to isolate teachers in their classrooms, so the traditional structure of school has discouraged teachers from being leaders. Within most schools, the leader's job is reserved for the principal, or for his or her assistants. Teachers may occasionally take on extra responsibilities, or assignments, but they rarely help to set policy, or give direction or advice to others. Indeed, because leadership often involves stepping outside traditional boundaries, or blazing new paths, leadership is activity discouraged in many schools. Teachers who try to lead are often viewed as misfits or squeaky wheels.

Next Century Schools typically allow teachers to carve out much bigger roles for themselves, by giving them greater leadership tasks. Sometimes, leadership is formalized—for example, when an individual is given a title such as project coordinator, or mentor teacher. More often, leadership is conferred on an ad hoc basis, as groups are formed to help set goals or address specific issues. At other times, leadership is completely informal, as when certain teachers become the custodians of information (troubleshooting the computers, for example) or the reference points for decisions (what materials should be covered in the math or science program). However it expresses itself, leadership among teachers usually flows from a principal or superintendent who trusts his team and delegates real responsibility to them.

At West Forest Intermediate School in Opelika, Alabama, for example, Principal Cheryl Deaton has nurtured many leaders among her staff. Although everyone concedes that West Forest "marches to Dr. Deaton's beat," there are many individuals who have shaped the school's program. Reorganized into a set of schools within the school (based on a space theme), West Forest has created roles for many leaders. For example, Betty Wingo is the coordinator of the program's special education services, and is the lead teacher for one of the "dimensions," a grouping of approximately one hundred students. Anita Meadows coordinates the media center and is responsible for implementation of technology throughout the program. Suzanne Meadows handles the implementation of the whole-language program. For her part, Dr. Deaton wishes she had delegated even more. "If we had it to do over again," she says, "I would allow more staff members to take leadership roles in developing elements of the new program."

At Denali Elementary in Fairbanks, Alaska, enhanced science instruction forms the core of the school's NCS program. The sparkplug of this effort is Ruthanne Rust, a veteran teacher who has been designated mentor science teacher. Ruthanne spends the majority of her time working one-on-one with other teachers, as well as managing the Discovery Room, which is used by teachers, students, and parents. She says, "My role is to stir up science. I know I have three years to work with this staff. Ideally, in three years, I shouldn't be needed here."

In a few cases, the leadership from a teacher can be so

powerful that it can transform the school. At Douglas Byrd Junior High, Rosie Bullard helped to design and then implement the STAR program for drop-out-prone seventh-graders. Despite initial resistance from the school principal, Rosie's persistent energy and enthusiasm not only made the program succeed, it gradually changed attitudes and behavior throughout the school, and spawned similar efforts in nearby schools.

Historically, teachers with leadership capabilities have had only one option: to pursue the administrative track lined with education and management courses to become a principal or a district administrator. These jobs in the bureaucracy often turn out to be stifling for their occupants, as well as for those who report to them. But when teachers are given power and authority within schools, not only do they welcome it and thrive on it, they often produce spectacular results for the teachers and students they work with.

6. TEACHERS AS LEARNERS.

What should a teacher know and be able to do? Most schools of education answer this question with a numbing array of courses in educational philosophy, psychology, and child development. District and state bureaucracies duly require teachers to complete some minimum number of these jargon-mastery classes, and then establish boards to certify the results. In most districts, of course, students who graduate from schools of education must spend at least a few months as practice teachers in the classroom, where their real understanding of teaching begins.

Later, the process of formal skill development continues with "in-service training." In most public schools, this consists of obligatory sessions or courses specified by the district or the state, and endured by teachers. Across the country, on any given afternoon after school, heads are nodding and papers being traded as teachers sit through another boring training session, designed with the best intentions to improve their skills in the classroom.

While it would be unfair to condemn all of these programs as useless, most teachers would concede that their formal education as teachers has been less valuable than the skills they have acquired from experience, and from other teachers. The chief problem with most teacher-training programs parallels the problems with public schools themselves: They are not driven by concern for the client, but are designed by well-intentioned bureaucrats from outside the schools. Teachers seldom are allowed to decide what they need to know, or whom they should be taught by.

Many Next Century Schools have turned this process inside out. A striking number have included staff development in their budgets and their plans for change. This desire to invest in their staffs has been fueled by a realization that it is not possible to transform an institution such as a school without changing the behavior, the knowledge, and the attitudes of teachers. But in nearly every case, it is teachers themselves who have decided what education they need, and how they should acquire it.

At Franklin Junior High, the teachers select the seminars or courses they will attend across the state, and then report back to others. (Parents are invited to these instructional activities as well.) At New Stanley, the teachers collectively decided which issues they wanted to explore during the second year of the program, and then assigned one of their members to identify and recruit the right instructors for their program. At Bloomfield Hills in Michigan, the teachers began

160

their planning process with a wide-ranging survey of educational research. Now that their program has been defined, they maintain an extensive library that covers issues such as personal learning plans, teacher-coaching strategies, and alternative assessment approaches.

Many schools have developed strong relationships with local universities, as one source of advice and instruction. At Piscataquis, for example, the change process has been mentored by Russ Quaglia, a professor whose exciting "Models for Change" class was chosen by teachers as the basis for their planning retreats.

At trailblazing schools like Bloomfield Hills, New Stanley, The Downtown School, and Davis, the teachers have become instructors of other teachers. In the first two years of their programs, as word of their success spread, the teachers in these schools hosted hundreds of visitors, and responded to dozens of requests to share their acquired expertise with others in the district and the state. For Davis, a partial answer was to develop a video program that could explain Recess Math in a few minutes. At Union House Elementary in Sacramento, California, a student-produced video gives a child's-eye view of the changes under way. Others have created structured presentations that capture the important elements of their programs, or have written documentation that can be adapted by others.

The message from Next Century Schools can be simply summarized: Teachers are avid learners, if they are put in charge of their own education. Staff development plays a critical part in the reform process, but this development must be designed and run by teachers themselves.

7. TEACHERS AS AUTHORS.

In most public schools, basic textbooks and course objectives are specified by state bureaucrats, based on guidance by the chief state school officer and the state board of education. These intensely political decisions typically leave no one satisfied, and often produce committee-written course materials that are insipid and dull. Trying to excite young minds with such stultifying materials is a daunting challenge. Many teachers wish that this unfortunate reality could be changed. Even though many teachers select supplemental books or videos to enliven their courses, or branch out with self-developed texts, the typical teacher lacks the money, time, and freedom to develop new curriculum materials.

A few Next Century Schools, however, have used grant funds to undertake major projects in curriculum development. For example, at Linda Vista Elementary in San Diego, the need to teach children from many cultures has forced teachers to acquire and develop new materials in many languages. At Bloomfield Hills, several teachers have developed interdisciplinary course materials in history and English. At Beeber Middle School in Philadelphia, Pennsylvania, students helped to develop courses in subjects of direct interest to them.

Two of the most innovative and far-reaching efforts at curriculum development in Next Century Schools involve the use of interactive computers to deliver instruction. At Orem High School in Orem, Utah, a team of teachers is creating an interactive course that combines advanced algebra with chemistry and technical writing. Although the software is still being debugged by software engineers from the University of Utah, the course is already being taught to tenth-graders at the school. If it succeeds, the course might be used to instruct students in many settings in and out of school, and could even be adapted for home use. Importantly, all of the course materials, questions, illustrations, and tests were developed entirely by a team of teachers from the school, rather than by outside experts.

Across the country, a similar effort is under way at Rappahannock Elementary School in Sperryville, Virginia. Here, teachers, along with experts from companies such as Xerox and Potomac Electric, are developing an interactive computer program intended to teach math, social studies, and science to fourth-graders. This radical approach to curriculum not only combines several disciplines, it is intended to change the role of the teacher from knowledge-provider to course-developer and guide.

Although most teachers are unlikely to become authors of their own texts or software, many have the interest and the talent to do so. As computers become more ubiquitous and more seamlessly tied together, teachers (and students) are more likely to be able to contribute their own course materials, embellishments, and improvements to educators in other schools. Ultimately, curriculum development may become a continuous process that is highly individualized and accessible to many teachers. Rather than continuing to be centralized in the hands of a few expert textbook authors, curriculum development may be controlled by teachers.

8. Teachers of the Future.

Where do innovative and competent teachers come from today, and where will the next century's teachers be found? Periodically, news stories report a looming teacher shortage, as retirements, pay gaps, and changing career expectations among women threaten to constrain the numbers of new people entering the profession.

In light of these negative trends, the remarkable record of teachers in Next Century Schools is even more surprising. With rare exceptions, the teachers who are performing so unusually and so successfully in these schools are a cross-section of the more than two million public school teachers across the country. To judge by the thousands of similar proposals made by other teachers and principals to the RJR Nabisco Foundation, there are tens of thousands more who are equally competent, dedicated, and enthusiastic, waiting for their energies to be tapped and harnessed more successfully.

But in recent years, the apparent quality of those choosing to enter schools of education has declined. And the obstacles to recruiting outside the traditional sources are formidable. Although most Next Century Schools had little trouble finding talented people to staff their experiments, the experience of one principal illustrates how tight the straitjacket is around innovators seeking to hire talented professionals in the schools.

Charles Dluzniewski, the principal of Nathan Hale Middle School, in Brooklyn, New York, is a dedicated, caring, and canny administrator, struggling against a difficult environment. Despite the drugs, guns, and violence that sometimes plague his school and his neighborhood, he has managed to make his school an oasis of learning amid extremely unfavorable conditions. But when Dluzniewski wanted to hire an assistant, he faced a set of bureaucratic hurdles that Kafka might have imagined. As Dluzniewski describes the three-step process:

> First, my teacher selection committee and I had to interview approximately fifteen to twenty candidates,

balanced by race, ethnicity, and gender, all of whom had to have the right certifications and coursework. The interviews lasted about an hour each, after which we had to summarize our impressions in writing, and select the top five candidates. We could not indicate which candidate we preferred, but simply had to submit the names to the next level.

Next, my school management board, which consists of eleven parents, community leaders, and others interviewed the five candidates. Many of these board members have no real knowledge of education, or the demands of this job, but each one had a vote in the process. The board ranked, and sent forward three names to the superintendent.

Finally, the superintendent is supposed to select the person he wants to be my assistant principal. The whole process has taken about a year, and I still don't know who my deputy will be.

Although New York's rules exaggerate the mindlessness of the staff selection process, it is symptomatic of a system in which procedures and credentials have replaced logic and common sense.

Still, Next Century Schools have managed not only to find cadres of excellent teachers from within the system, they have found ways to reach outside the system for talent. And in selecting talent, they have typically gone beyond the profile of the typical teacher, to find people with varying skills that would make a difference with kids. At Chelsea, Maggie Lodge found a way to reach drop-outs with George Roman, a former drop-out, by upgrading his responsibilities from security to counseling. At John Marshall, in Los Angeles, David Tokofsky, a government teacher, brings lawyers from O'Melveny and Myers to stage mock trials and collective bargaining negotiations, and to arrange internships for students. At Linda Vista Elementary, Adel Nadeau, the principal, has recruited teachers who speak Vietnamese and Hmong to reach her students in their native languages. In Utah, Orem High reached into Brigham Young University to find programming and instructional design talent to supplement the work of its full-time teachers.

These nontraditional teachers illustrate a simple principle: Competent teachers, with a variety of skills, are still willing to work in public schools that are well-managed. Teachers will flock to schools that are led by motivated, energetic leaders, with a serious commitment to educating young people. Although eroding teacher pay and inflexible salary scales may ultimately create a crisis of competence in public school teaching, the lesson from Next Century Schools is that good leaders can still find good teachers.

Teacher Unions

Teachers' new roles will lead to new relationships with teacher unions. In contrast to the broad decline in union membership in most industries, unions have organized the great majority of teachers in the nation's large school districts over the past fifteen years. In 1977 the Teamsters were the nations largest union; today that honor is held by the National Education Association.

But despite grumbling from school administrators over pay demands, and complaints by school reformers over union intransigence, the record of Next Century Schools suggests that unions are not a significant obstacle to change in most places. Indeed, there are many examples in which union leaders have been instrumental in reform efforts.

Next Century Schools seem to bear out the adage sometimes applied in other industries: Management gets the unions it deserves. Among Next Century Schools, those operating in environments with traditionally hostile union-management relationships have struggled and debated over even modest changes. In one case a school that was included in the final selection round was unable to submit a final proposal because of union objections to the reforms. At Chelsea High School the Pathways program has been attacked in court for violating union hiring rules.

But in other cases, union leaders have been architects of reform proposals. In most cases, school administrators have actively sought union input and ideas from the early planning stages. And typically this attitude of partnership has led to positive responses from local union leaders. After all, most reform programs involve empowerment of teachers, shared decision-making, and greater flexibility for those in the classroom, ideas that are welcomed among rank-and-file teachers.

In some cases, reform has been the object of bold collective bargaining agreements. In Memphis, for example, the NEA negotiated an agreement that included pay differentials, and wholesale reshuffling of teacher assignments to promote radical improvements in struggling inner city schools.

Unions and collective bargaining are facts of American public education, just as they are present elsewhere in American industry. But while unions may demand a voice in reform efforts, they need not be obstacles to change. One of the most pressing issues before the nation is reforming teacher pay. After years of slow pay gains, teachers enjoyed significant wage increases in the late 1980s. But despite the improvements, teacher pay systems are still antiquated. Unlike professionals with similar educations, teachers are paid more like factory workers than skilled professionals. In most districts, the best teachers and the worst are paid the same. Differences in performance, skills, disciplines, or competitive conditions matter not at all. Like the factories after which public schools are modeled, schools pay teachers based primarily on seniority, and on college credit hours beyond the bachelors degree.

The result of this blindly egalitarian system is both low average pay, and chronic shortages in certain disciplines. For example, North Carolina reports there are only eleven teachers in the state certified to teach advanced physics. The problem is not a shortage of physics teachers but of common sense. If physics teachers were paid competitively, there would be an adequate supply. But at present, men and women who by temperament and training would make fine physics teachers will not present themselves to teach physics because the conditions of work, certification requirements, and compensation are not competitive with the other opportunities they have.

Until teachers are paid as other professionals, according to variations in the labor market, schools will face growing difficulty maintaining the quality of their workforce. As teachers retire, and young women choose higher paying fields that are opening to them, teacher quality may drop.

Although sensitivity to market conditions is important, it is equally urgent that pay be linked to performance. Like other professionals, teacher pay must be tied to results. This includes both individual success in the classroom, and the overall success of the school. There may be no perfect merit-pay system for teachers, and the issue is certain to be divisive. But teachers should be able to enjoy a reward for doing especially well with their own students, and should also share bonuses based in part on how well their colleagues are performing as a group. Pay, like other aspects of school management, must adjust to modern organizational realities.

Teachers today are the most poorly managed group of professionals in America. They operate within hierarchical systems that stifle initiative, thwart teamwork, limit creativity, and pay factory wages. But the professionals in Next Century Schools demonstrate that if teachers are given freedom to define their own goals, and the responsibility to make their own choices, they will perform magnificently. If teachers are treated like talented professionals, schools will operate far more effectively and productively. Again and again, visitors to Next Century Schools meet teachers with similar stories. After years of frustration and boredom, they were ready to leave the profession. But the new program and new leadership have revitalized their attitudes and reinvigorated their dedication. As Betty Wingo at West Forest Intermediate put it, "We can never go back. This is the most incredible thing I've ever been a part of."

One of the most basic lessons of modern management is that to obtain the full benefits of an educated workforce, responsibility must be delegated throughout the organization. Schools of the next century will be run by teams of teachers, who are given the tools, incentives, and leadership they need to accomplish their jobs. When communities can accomplish this, they will be astounded by the results.

CHAPTER 7

What Should We Expect of Students?

Perhaps the most valuable result of all education is the ability to make yourself do the thing you have to do, when it ought to be done, whether you like it or not; it is the first lesson that ought to be learned; and however early a man's training begins, it is probably the last lesson that he learns thoroughly.

—Thomas Henry Huxley,
Technical Education

Too little is expected of American students, and as a consequence too little is delivered. Adults expect too little from them; students expect too little of themselves. That is why American kids do not compare favorably to kids in other parts of the world. As a society we should expect more of students—much more. We do them no favor by letting them "get by." In the future, students must become workers, not shirkers.

We should expect more from students than just book learning. Education is more than knowledge; it includes attitudes and competencies as well. Schools help shape attitudes toward work, toward friends and colleagues, and toward self, in both the regular academic program and in the nonacademic program.

There are several, interconnected parts to the life of the successful student, each reflected in Next Century Schools:

- Academic knowledge—the core curriculum which all students must master as a condition of graduation;

- Attitudes toward work, community, school, colleagues, and self—a willingness to work and work hard; honesty and loyalty; diligence and attention to detail; a willingness to sacrifice for the common good and for personal accomplishment; capacity to serve school and community; and the capacity to take pleasure in the opportunities life affords;

- A capacity to participate constructively in the life of the school, as advocate, critic, and worker; and,

- A capacity to move into postsecondary education, work, and community and civic affairs.

Today, students attend and participate in the life of the school by the luck of the draw. Enrolled on the basis of neighborhoods, students are required by compulsory attendance statutes to go to school; they study as the spirit moves them. No wonder so many do so poorly. With little motivation, weak incentives, and few rewards, it is the rare student who is truly diligent.

By way of contrast, many American students are among the best in the world at the college, university, postgraduate, and professional level. How can that be? The difference is that after high school there are incentives for performance, particularly among those who wish to pursue focused, high-status careers. The youngster who hopes to teach in an Ivy League college, practice medicine, join a prestigious law firm, or become an architect, a business leader, or a senior civil servant must learn early that it pays to be a good student.

However, unlike European and Asian students, relatively few American students realize this while in high school. This phenomenon is in large part the result of one of America's greatest virtues: We are a land of second chances.

In Europe, for example, failure in a small business is a disaster; in America, although it is painful and sobering, it hap-

174

pens so often that analysts today see it is as a difficult but
often necessary first step. The high rate of small business
"failure" is an important part of the school of hard knocks.
Indeed, so often did Thomas Edison "fail" that he didn't use
the word: Discussing his long and tortuous path to the development of the incandescent light bulb, Edison dryly noted
that he "had learned a lot about bulbs that do not work."

As many know, failure is one of our most potent
teachers—at least for the determined and disciplined. Failure is the hallmark of the scientific method; failures permit
the scientist to dismiss and discard wrong paths. We learn
from failure, and serious students, particularly late bloomers,
can go back again and again until they finally get it right.

But for all the kids who understand that failure may be a
prelude to success, there are the kids who don't understand
its significance. As Lee Iaccoca said in a speech to the National Education Association:

> We've lost something else in many of our schools be-
> sides discipline. We've lost the value of failure. The
> first thing some youngsters flunk these days is life it-
> self. That's because they've been passed from one
> grade to another, and eventually graduated, even
> though they've been failing at every step. The only
> problem is, nobody's told them. In attempting to
> shield these kids from failure, we've guaranteed it.

For every kid who profits from failure there are the kids
who don't bounce back. They believe that failure is terminal,
not a way station. They drop out and stay out. One failure in
school crushes them. Even for those resilient kids who do
bounce back, the recovery is expensive and time-consuming;
better to do it right the first time.

Nowhere do we see this more clearly than in education. According to school data, more than 25 percent of all high school students drop out; yet when census data for twenty-year-olds is examined, it turns out that about half of those who were first counted as drop-outs have dropped back in. Some have earned GED diplomas, some have returned to alternate schools, and others have gone directly to junior or community college. A small number go on to four-year institutions without a high school diploma, while others have found vocational or technical training programs that put them into the workforce.

There are even important programs in place designed to facilitate the process. In California, for example, passing the California High School Proficiency Examination (CHSPE) permits you to go straight to junior college or a four-year institution without earning a high school diploma. The program was originally sold as a way to increase the efficiency of the state system of funding lower and higher education; State Department of Finance analysts hoped it would save money for the state as a whole by moving abled youngsters along more rapidly.

Minnesota is home to an even more daring idea. A provision in state law that permits a youngster who secures early admission at a state college or university to keep his or her state and local funds, money that would otherwise be spent on high school, and apply them to college tuition. Although the program is only a few years old, the results are striking. Youngsters who leave high school early to attend college do better in their freshman year than their college classmates who completed high school.

In Europe and Asia, youngsters who fail to do well in secondary school, however, fail outright. They have no second chance, except in the narrowest sense. In Japan, secondary school graduates who fail their university entrance examinations and study for a second try even have a special name—*ronin*—the historical term for a samurai without a master.

How are kids motivated to "do it right the first time"? Abroad, colleges and universities are available only to the best students. From an early age, students know that their life chances will be determined by how well they perform in elementary and secondary school. They behave the way our best young athletes do—training diligently and investing long hours and hard work in the process of self-improvement. This was once true of academic effort in America. Until the modern era, colleges and universities were the gatekeepers of quality. Their entrance standards set the exit standards for secondary schools. The whole concept of Carnegie units was designed to let students know what was expected of them across a very diverse country. Carnegie units were a turn-of-the-century reform, named after philanthropist Andrew Carnegie. Units were assigned to academic courses—a proxy for both time and degree of difficulty—and a student who hoped to attend college or university found it necessary to accumulate a required number of Carnegie units. With few exceptions, higher education institutions established similar Carnegie unit requirements. Although the requirements changed over time, the core changed little. College-bound high school students were expected to take four years of English, three of math and science, two of a foreign language, and the like. Carnegie units revealed the distribution of courses a student took. Thus, a college or university would require that certain courses be taken in specified sequences. The Carnegie unit became a national metric, which all higher education institutions were familiar with and which permitted kids from very different backgrounds to be compared.

There were limits to Carnegie units, however, particularly when considering poor and isolated communities that were less rigorous or unable to offer a full range of college preparation courses. With this shortcoming in mind, the Scholastic Aptitude Test was born. More recently, SATs have been supplemented by Achievement tests and Advanced Placement examinations. But not even this complex set of filters for college entry has kept entry standards, and consequently, high school leaving standards, high and rigorous. If anything, they are lower today than they were a few decades ago. What has happened? There are three things to keep in mind:

- America's best colleges and universities are still the envy of the world. No other country has anything that remotely compares, not even Europe as a whole. The best American higher education is still the world standard.

- Not only do we have the best, we have the most higher education institutions. With 3,500 postsecondary institutions, America has one-third of the world's supply.

- With the best and the most, we also have some of the least challenging. Only about 100 of the best institutions are seriously selective; the vast majority are essentially open-enrollment institutions, junior and community colleges, trade and technical schools, and adult education centers.

The extraordinarily high quality of America's best colleges and universities is well known throughout the world. Thousands of students from across the globe study at America's best institutions; thousands of our best teachers are foreign-born as well. Both of these phenomena demonstrate

178

just how good the best American schools are. Yet only a small fraction of Americans actually attend demanding, selective institutions.

If American higher education includes the best, we also have an abundant supply of second- and even third-rate institutions, putting students in a buyer's market; the oversupply of higher education seats means that institutions are furiously competing with each other for a vast student pool.

Ironically, we are witnessing two trends at work simultaneously, one of which has a pernicious effect on student behavior in high school. The number of higher education institutions has exploded since the Second World War and on a relative scale, quality has not kept pace with quantity. The good news is that never has higher education been so accessible to so many. The bad news is the quality is not what it should be.

Once college was important only for those who wanted to join the learned professions—prospective teachers, doctors, lawyers, accountants, architects, and clerics. It was possible to make a decent, even a very comfortable, living without having gone to college. Particularly in an industrial economy with strong unions and generous benefit and job-protection programs, academic achievement had little financial payoff for those kids who were going straight to the workplace. For kids fortunate enough to land jobs in unionized industries, they could find skilled work that paid more than college teaching. This is no longer the case.

What of the youngster who has little or no interest in college, the youngster at risk of dropping out and never returning? A number of Next Century Schools are concerned with precisely that population.

No school has a more inventive or straightforward solution than Carl Sandburg Intermediate School in Alexandria,

Virginia. In examining their record of accomplishment, Carl Sandburg's staff had much to be proud of; 88 percent of their graduates went on to high school and did well. However, they had much to be concerned about as well. Twelve percent of their graduates did not do well, a number significantly higher than in their school district as a whole. Although the staff at Sandburg didn't use the term, they were borrowing one of business's most powerful practices: benchmarking. They were looking at the competition, other schools in their system, to see how they were doing. The comparison was unsettling. They weren't doing as well as they should have been.

Instead of blaming the students, as too many schools do, the staff at Sandburg decided to do something. First they got the facts. They studied the kids who weren't making the transition to high school successfully and found that they exhibited similar traits: high absenteeism, low attention in class (when they were there), and infrequent efforts to do, let alone complete, homework. The problem Sandburg confronted was how to turn these kids into workers. No one else could do the work for them. You couldn't hold them down or tie them up and fill them with knowledge. They had to learn it themselves, the old-fashioned way. But the old-fashioned incentives to work hard did not work, and it did no good to wring your hands and complain.

The old environment had not done the trick. To use the language of the modern firm, Sandburg was not meeting customer requirements. Whatever was going on at Sandburg left out 12 percent of the kids. Indeed, the lesson of the modern economy is that any number of kids, even 1 percent, is too big to leave out.

Sandburg uses the promise of TV time, in the school studio, to engage youngsters who are at risk of dropping out. By way of contrast, Brunswick Acres School in New Jersey has initiated peer tutoring, one of the most promising and inexpensive interventions available to schools. In this case, sixth-graders are assigned to tutor elementary-age children as well as handicapped youngsters in the preschool program. One of the most successful tutors was a child with a history of acting up. Surprising? Only superficially. Tutoring does as much for the tutor as for the student being tutored. Other strategies work as well. DeAnza Junior High School in Calexico, California, on the Mexican border, finds that computers exert a magnetic appeal. Students literally queue up outside the computer labs to get time on the machines before the beginning of the regular school day. So excited—and so motivated—are the students that they have taken it upon themselves to organize access to the computers, patiently waiting in line—without adult supervision—for their time on the computer.

Instructional devices that capitalize on the "teachable moments" are numerous, even endless, limited only by the ingenuity of teachers and students. What is needed is the right setting.

The solution? Clearly stated standards and measures (curriculum and tests), and incentives to achieve them, and rewards once they are achieved. At Sandburg the standards were already in place. What was needed were incentives and rewards like the chance to work in the school's TV studio. At Sandburg, work is a reward for work. If a student shows up, does the homework, and pays attention in class, then he or she will earn the opportunity to work after school. Does the Sandburg approach work? Although the jury is still out, it should work—that's what the NCS program is all about: bold experiments. The staff, as they should, is convinced their program will succeed.

As the example of Sandburg reveals, there is more than

one way to ask more of students, parents, and teachers. The logic of asking more of elementary- and secondary-school students means that more must be expected of them as they make college and work plans.

Even if we cannot fully restore the role of gatekeeper and arbiter of standards to colleges and universities in its entirety, we can still expect students to master their secondary-school work. A certificate of attendance is not enough. School should not be simply a test of endurance.

In addition, other pressure points should be applied from the community, and from public, not-for-profit and private institutions. Though the nation's workforce is well over 125 million workers, it is rare for an employer to ask to see a student's transcript of record to make a judgment about qualifications and competence. Yet the idea is not farfetched. A story, perhaps apocryphal, makes the point. The retailing giant JC Penney used to counsel store managers about interviewing prospective clerks: If the youngster being interviewed has a high school diploma and wears a Future Farmers of America or 4-H jacket, he or she is a good bet. No doubt they were, and still are.

The example points out the importance of proxies for achievement and competence; a kid with an adequate high school diploma and a demonstrated work record on a farm or ranch is a good bet. Unfortunately, we have few such proxies in the nonfarm world. The Committee for Economic Development in its policy statement, *Investing in Our Children,* recommended that transcripts be routinely used to evaluate prospective employees. Employers should look not only at grades, but at written material that would give the interviewer some better feeling for what the young person knows and is able to do. In New Zealand, youngsters have portfolios that document school and extracurricular activities. The approach makes sense. This, after all, is how we judge people in the workplace. We don't give grades to employees as schools do. Rather, before making hiring or promotion decisions, we review the résumé and recommendations; observe the quality and quantity of their work; note their interpersonal skills; compare them to other employees doing similar work; and, make a judgment about their attitude and competence.

What Should Schools Teach?

What does mastery mean and what should students master? Before these questions can be answered, there must be some agreement on the basic purposes of public education. While there are many differences on details, most Americans believe that public education should prepare young people for three roles: citizens of a democracy, workers in a complex economy, and participants in the larger society.

In a great democracy, education's first task is to prepare people for the responsibilities and opportunities of citizenship. As James Madison said in a letter to W. T. Berry in 1822:

Knowledge will forever govern ignorance: and a people who mean to be their own governors, must arm themselves with the power which knowledge gives.

Equally importantly, education should prepare people for work, laying the academic foundations that permit individuals to acquire the skills, knowledge, and attitudes they need to be successful. As the skills required by our economy have risen, along with the wages of the best-educated people, the economic importance of education has increased for our society and for individuals. Finally, education should prepare people to participate in the larger society, to use leisure time constructively, to give of themselves, and to derive satisfaction and pleasure from their accomplishments and efforts.

These purposes are not in conflict with each other but are increasingly closely related. The ability to read and understand and to articulate a point of view is essential whether one is participating in the political process or supervising a work team. Knowledge of math is important whether you are buying a car, measuring a child's medicine, or shopping at the supermarket.

Although businesspeople have been accused of wanting to refocus public education strictly on work-related skills, in fact, business increasingly needs broadly educated individuals. Today, at least, education for citizenship and for personal fulfillment is much the same as education for economic life, because the skills and knowledge you need are the same. The qualities that make a good worker in the modern firm are the same as those that make a good citizen: respect for others, initiative, the capacity to communicate clearly and directly, willingness to take risks while playing by the rules, energy, dedication, and knowledge. Our common curriculum should include the national goals enunciated in 1990 by President Bush and the governors: English, geography, history, mathematics, science, a second language. It should also include the arts, physical education and health, and community service.

Most important of all is mastery of English, which cuts across the curriculum as a whole. Left-wing critics assert that requiring English is a form of cultural imperialism. Such charges are nonsense. Call it American English if you like, but we must all speak the same language. Ours is a great continental common market, and a common language is essential to its success. Noah Webster, lexicographer and patriot, recognized this when he released his first dictionary of American English in the 1830s. His path-breaking effort was as much an exercise in nation-building as in lexicography, and we would do well to emulate him today. A common language is not jingoism; it is eminently practical and useful.

But a common language means more than mastery of English; it includes a shared understanding of culture, habits, customs, and behavior. Many things knit us together, from shared experiences and a common democratic vision to pop culture, including sports, entertainment, comics, even brand names. Try to imagine America without Ford Motors, Mark Twain, Coca-Cola, Hollywood, the New York Yankees, Kleenex, Levis, Michael Jordan, Xerox, or Mickey Mouse. Our cultural icons, our biggest export, help define us as a people, and our shared knowledge of them makes it possible for us to talk to one another.

Oddly, for all of America's widely noted frontier tradition, and its abiding commitment to local control, the question of what should be taught seems to be largely predetermined in most school systems. Indeed, although it is informal, a *de facto* national curriculum already exists. Of course, national politicians decry the notion of a national curriculum and praise the idea of local self-determination, but the truth is that America already has a tightly defined set of courses and materials that are taught in the vast majority of public schools.

With 50 states and several trust territories, with more than 15,500 independent school districts, more than 110,000 public and private school buildings, more than 80,000 school board members, and more than 7,500 state legislators, one would expect hundreds, even thousands of different curricula. But the more carefully one examines the curricular offerings of thousands of schools spread across the continent, the more alike they look.

America's schools—public and private, North and South, East and West, rural and urban, rich and poor, academic, general track, and vocational—are much more alike than dissimilar. Even fast-paced examination schools, like Bronx Science or Stuyvesant in New York, or NCS winners like the North Carolina School of Science and Math or Moon Valley in Arizona, offer a "common" curriculum that looks like the schools of Boise, Idaho, Portland, Maine, or Austin, Texas. Indeed, one of the most interesting aspects of Next Century Schools—all forty-two of them, from Alaska to Florida—is how similar their curricula are. Most high schools offer four years of English, three or four years of mathematics through algebra II and calculus, three years of science, including biology, chemistry, and physics, and two or more years of history.

These courses reflect a desire to impart a shared set of ideas and information. There are, of course, differences of emphasis. The Denali school in Fairbanks, Alaska, for example, stresses the role and importance of Native American culture as the entry point for studying ecology, which is itself the point of entry for introductory biology, botany, chemistry, physics, and math. The Ortega school in Austin, Texas, uses its special characteristics and ethnic composition as the point of departure for academic study. Most of the students are Hispanic, with close linguistic and cultural ties to Mexico, and Ortega uses this as a way to widen student horizons—Hispanic themes stimulate student interest. But in each case the fundamental curriculum is the same; what's different is the details. At the level of basic concepts and knowledge, then, we already have an informal national core curriculum.

Textbook selection reinforces the national curriculum. A handful of major publishers provides the books and tests that the vast majority of students use, and a few states— most notably, California, Florida, Texas, and New York— dominate the market by the size of their purchases. The effect is to provide the content for a national curriculum. Together with college entrance tests, the textbook market has defined what, when, and how most high school students learn.

The issue of curriculum—what youngsters should know and be able to do—has special importance in settings where questions of cultural diversity arise. In no school is this issue raised more sharply than Tuba City High School in Tuba City, Arizona, where nearly 100 percent of the enrollment is Navajo. Tuba City students have a unique cultural tradition of which they are justifiably proud, yet it is also essential for them to be fully educated in the "national" curriculum to permit them to take their place in the national culture and economy. They've used their Next Century Schools grant with that in mind. The high school is divided into career-focused "houses," or small units in which students and teachers work together, creating closer bonds, greater continuity, and accountability—all of which helps keep students on the right track.

Goals for the Next Century

If a *de facto* national curriculum already exists, what areas should local schools focus on in setting new goals? Next Century Schools and other education reformers give at least three answers to this question:

- Existing standards for mastering the traditional curriculum must be raised, and applied to all children.

- The curriculum must reflect the importance of skills that will be useful in the workplace.

- The courses that the school teaches must be supplemented by more emphasis on teaching (largely by example) personal values, attitudes, and behaviors such as deportment, honesty, punctuality, and civility.

Measuring Mastery by Levels of Accomplishment

"Every child can learn." This is one of the most often repeated clichés of American public education. It is true that all normal children are capable of mastering difficult material and achieving at high standards, but public schools seldom realize this goal. Limited resources for re-teaching slow learners or for individualizing instruction, lock-step grade levels, widely different student backgrounds and aptitudes, and uneven parental involvement virtually guarantee that in most public schools, some children learn a lot, some learn a little, and some fail. Schools and teachers who have witnessed this reality over many years have come to expect it and to set their expectations accordingly. Gradually, standards have eroded, especially for students from disadvantaged backgrounds.

With the growing demand for higher skills on the job, an increasing number of schools have recognized that they cannot continue to tolerate such uneven academic performance. Accordingly, many reform-minded schools have rededicated themselves to ensuring that all children reach minimum levels of academic competency. In practice, this new attention to upgrading the performance of students who historically have done poorly requires a fundamental overhaul in teaching.

At many schools, the goal of improving the performance of low-achievers has meant the creation of special afternoon or summer programs. At Piscataquis High School, in Guilford, Maine, however, this goal has led to a complete recasting of the traditional school day. Eliminating tracking and vocational courses forced the redesign of academic courses, based on achievement levels, permitting every student to reach higher levels of accomplishment. Piscataquis has decided to totally overhaul its curriculum to lower the failure rate among weaker students. Similarly, at New Stanley Elementary, in Kansas City, Kansas, the school's goal is "to raise the performance of every student at least to grade level." In order to do so, the school has moved to more individualized instruction, enlisted students to teach other students, allocated extra teaching time to help weaker students, and insisted that no grade below a B (indicating mastery of the material), is final. All other test results are deemed incomplete, and require continued effort by the teacher and the student.

For many schools, then, the challenge has not been to reform the basic "national" curriculum for college-bound students that has been in place for so many years across the country. Rather it has been to raise the standards for all students, including the minimum standards that are acceptable.

How high should minimum standards be set? The only honest answer is that "it all depends." It depends on what a student plans to do as an adult, on how hard the student is willing to work, and on what standards will be demanded in the workplace. Standards should be high and rigorous, but they should also be flexible. And they should be "mastery standards," not time-based—reflecting not hours or weeks studied but demonstrated accomplishment. In this way a student may achieve different levels of accomplishment at different times in his life.

For example, knowledge of typing is required to use computers. Well over half the nation's workforce now uses a keyboard at some point during the work week, and that number will increase (at least until the voice-activated computer becomes a reality). But if it is clear that everyone should learn how to use a keyboard, the question remains, how well? How fast and how accurately should an individual type? It all depends. If a student plans to become a production typist, 80 words a minute with 95 percent accuracy might be the right target. If he or she plans to be a journalist, 45 words a minute with 80 percent accuracy—with two fingers—will probably do. As a general rule, of course, the faster and more accurate the better, but there are limits. There is a point of diminishing returns in typing as there is in any enterprise. And the rule should simply be, Type as fast and as accurately as your tasks require and as your ambition leads you.

At a more sophisticated level, consider the rating scale for measuring language proficiency used by the Foreign Service Language Institute, the Defense Language Institute, and most other modern language schools. Instead of reporting that a student attended school for a finite time and received a certain grade, student mastery is reported on a scale of 0 to 5+, ranging from no knowledge of a language—0—to simultaneous translator ability, with a degree of fluency equal to a native speaker—5+. Knowledge sufficient to meet the needs of a commercial attache might be a 3; to teach the language, a 4+; to speak with the ease and fluency of a sophisticated native speaker, a 5; and to get around Paris, Rome, or Tokyo as a tourist, a 1+. The power of this approach is immediately apparent; it is an international language of its own, understandable across cultural and geographic boundaries. It also disconnects "learning" and "school"; native speakers (foreign-born or not) or self-taught learners may "test out." In this respect, the language scale is similar to the Advanced Placement examinations of the Education Testing Service, which also uses a 0 to 5 scale, and reveals mastery rather than time served.

These examples suggest that there is no absolute skill level, no single point of ultimate mastery. Rather, mastery occurs on a continuum; for educational accomplishment, schools should adopt the approach of the National Assessment of Educational Progress, which uses a continuous numerical scale, and defines several levels of accomplishment: basic, adept, and advanced. Clearly, all students should achieve at least a "basic" level in every major curriculum area. Beyond this level, every student should be challenged to advance as far as possible. Such an approach eliminates the traditional adherence to an outmoded set of "input measures": how many hours a day or week a student goes to school; how many books he has read; how many teachers hold advanced degrees; how much money the school spends per pupil. Rather it substitutes "outputs"—what students gain as a consequence of attending school—and measures results on a continuous, extendable scale. To be meaningful, the standards must be keyed to national standards, and must be certified by authentic assessments.

Integrating Workplace Skills

Our *de facto* national curriculum was designed largely for the college-bound student. But not all students will go on to college. An alternative approach to the question of basic goals has been to focus attention on the skills all students will need to succeed in the workplace regardless of the

191

length of their education, or the type of job they may have. In 1991 the U.S. Department of Labor issued a report—SCANS (Secretary's Committee on Necessary Skills)—that outlined the types of workplace-related skills that all students should know. These included the abilities to:

- *Manage Resources:* productively allocate time, money, materials, space, or staff.

- *Work with Others:* cooperate with a team, teach others, serve customers, lead, negotiate, and work with diverse men and women.

- *Organize and Manage Information:* use computers and electronic telecommunications hardware and software.

- *Work with Complex Systems:* understand how technical, social, and organizational systems work, monitor and correct their performance, and design new systems to improve performance.

- *Work with a Variety of Technologies:* select appropriate tools, apply them to the tasks at hand, and maintain and trouble-shoot equipment.

Effective workers, the report argued, must also possess a foundation that includes:

- *Basic Skills:* reading, writing, mathematics (arithmetical computation and mathematical reasoning), listening, and speaking.

- *Thinking Skills:* creative thinking, decision-making, problem solving, seeing things in the mind's eye, knowing how to learn, and reasoning.

192

- *Personal Qualities:* individual responsibility, self-esteem, sociability, self-management, and integrity.

The report points out that most schools do not directly address many of these competencies or foundation skills. For example, creative thinking, working in groups, and the integration of technologies and tools are seldom part of traditional classroom work.

Some reform-minded schools have begun to address these concerns. For example, at Bloomfield Hills, Michigan, students are expected to develop portfolios that demonstrate their competence in a variety of skills, including those of value in the workplace.

Emphasizing the "Invisible" Curriculum

Alongside the "visible" curriculum—the program of courses the school offers—there is an "invisible" curriculum. It is invisible not because it cannot be seen, but because it is rarely taught directly, by teachers lecturing to students. To be effective it must be infused in the life of the school.

The invisible curriculum includes, but is not limited to, such things as deportment, demeanor, punctuality, civility, honesty, respect for self, and respect for others. These are the homespun virtues that schools must be concerned with, both as important messages to send students and as the basis of daily life.

Just as schools cannot run if students are not well-behaved, students cannot succeed in school—or life—if they fail to learn habits of self-restraint, forebearance, and delayed gratification. These are not just moral homilies, they are skills and values as basic as learning to count or to speak English.

How are these values taught and how are they learned?

By example and practice, rarely by study. Instead of lectures and catechisms, the most effective way to influence students is for the adults around them to be models of the behavior to which the kids should aspire.

Teachers who are proud of their calling and who take professional and personal satisfaction in their work, are the ones who leave a lasting impression on their students. And it is not just the knowledge—the "book learning"—they impart; it is the example they set. At Nathan Hale Elementary School in Brooklyn, New York, for example, one of the major goals of the Next Century School program was the creation of a more supportive, intimate, and positive tone among teachers and students. Only by first establishing an environment that reinforced the value of learning could the process of learning be accelerated. Similarly, at Douglas Byrd Junior High School in North Carolina, changes in the curriculum and the structure of classes were not as important as changing the expectations of students, parents, and teachers concerning behavior, attendance, and performance.

Increasing Motivation

How can we ensure that students embrace the curriculum? Using performance standards in which progression is based on progressively more difficult levels of mastery, and students complete prerequisites as a condition of advancement, will help to increase motivation.

One radical idea is to end compulsory attendance and replace it with the concept of guaranteed access. If students are not required to attend school after age fourteen, school becomes an opportunity which students must seize. But, everyone in the nation should be guaranteed access to a course of study which will lead, with hard work, to a diploma that means something.

Students Want High Standards Too

Students have been the missing link in the formation of school policies and the adoption of school practices. When they were treated as products on an assembly line, ignoring them may have been a source of irritation, but it was consistent with the rest of school life. If students are workers, however, the metaphor must be fully extended. Students deserve to be treated like thinking people, not products, and they should participate in the process of framing policy and practice. The process should be collaborative and cooperative, because everyone has something to gain.

The first thing that students can do is participate in serious discussion and debate. John Murphy, Superintendent of Charlotte-Mecklenburg, has pioneered this approach. In the spring of 1992, with the school system undergoing massive change and more proposed, Murphy assembled twenty juniors and seniors from each of CMS's thirteen high schools for a day-long symposium. A part of the opening session was a lecture about the state of American education; the balance of the day was devoted to student focus groups concluding with a plenary session in which the student focus groups presented their reports. The results? The students were harder on themselves and the schools than any other group in the community.

What did they want? Higher and more rigorous academic standards. Why? Because they were convinced that they were not being prepared to meet the competition. They knew they were not working as hard as they should, and they expected the adults around them to expect more of them. They also wanted an end to bonehead courses and mindless vocational courses. They were convinced that all students should be held to the same high standards. They called for an end to tracking. Instead, they argued that course completion should be determined by mastery, not time served, and that prerequisites should be met before advanced courses were taken.

What else did the students want? "Administrators with backbone" who would not tolerate drugs, alcohol, or violence on campus; teachers who made demands on students and who would be paid accordingly; teachers who would be disciplined, even fired, if they didn't cut it. These kids knew what the issues were and were prepared to speak out. Why hadn't they done so earlier? No one had ever asked them. And what is true in Charlotte is true across the country.

Expecting too little—something most people think of as wrong-headed but well-intentioned—actually works a cruel hoax on students. By expecting too little, students never get to stretch their wings; they never get to soar. They are denied the most profound pleasure of adult life—the sense of accomplishment provided by genuine mastery. The issue is not becoming as accomplished as Einstein, Shakespeare, Beethoven, or Michael Jordan; the issue is *becoming as accomplished as you can be.* None of us can be our best if we are not challenged. And this is the common thread among all Next Century Schools; in each of the forty-two sites, kids are challenged, rewarded, inspired. They reach higher than they ever thought they could.

CHAPTER 8

Beyond School: Parents and Community

From the wild Irish slums of the 19th century Eastern seaboard to the riot-torn suburbs of Los Angeles, there is one unmistakable lesson in American history: a community that allows a large number of young men to grow up in broken families, dominated by women, never acquiring any stable relationship to male authority, never acquiring any set of rational expectations about the future—that community asks for and gets chaos. Crime, violence, unrest, disorder—most particularly the furious, unrestrained lashing out at the whole social structure—that is not only to be expected, it is very near to inevitable. And it is richly deserved.

—from *America,* a Jesuit journal, September, 1965, quoted by Daniel Patrick Moynihan in "How the Great Society Destroyed the American Family," *The Public Interest,* Summer, 1992

As all students, parents, and teachers know, school can only do so much; even in the case of full-time students. From birth to age eighteen, schools command only 9 percent of a child's time. The other 91 percent is spent out of school. But all of that time has a direct bearing on schools. Children who get too little sleep—whether they watch too much TV or live in frightening, violence-prone neighborhoods—are children whose ability to learn is limited. On the other hand, children who grow up in tranquil homes where serious adult conversation is the norm are likely to learn more, faster.

In both a general and a specific sense, then, what children bring with them to school—not just knowledge, skills, and attitudes, but health and well-being—determines what they are able to learn. It also determines both what and how schools teach. Schools that fail to take into account the circumstances of their students will fail to reach them altogether, for what children bring to school varies greatly, school to school, child to child, era to era.

So obvious is the issue that it barely needs framing: Schools that receive children from advantaged, middle-class homes, children who are not only well-fed and well-cared for physically but who have been read to and attended to intellectually, face a very different challenge than schools who receive children from disadvantaged backgrounds. Teachers have been painfully aware of this truism throughout history. But its implications change as conditions change. In the late nineteenth century, Horace Mann, one of the founding fathers of modern public education, was concerned that the major problem before the public schools was to acculturate and socialize the two streams of migration that characterized the industrializing nation—internal migration from farm to factory and overseas migration to America.

Both waves of migration presented the schools of the day with challenges they were not well prepared to face; indeed, to this day it is not clear that they faced them humanely. Many kids were left out. But one thing is clear: Mann was able to marshal support for his growing common-school movement by advancing arguments about the importance of preparing these youngsters for the workplace. If this sounds familiar, it should: The more things change, the more they remain the same.

But if different children from different backgrounds is the common thread that runs through the common school, how is today different? In two important ways.

First, the nature of our economy has changed profoundly. No longer is ours an inward-looking domestic economy of farmers and factory workers. Our economy is global and high-tech, and there is no way to turn back the clock; to make an adequate living everyone must be well educated. The modern economy offers few options for the uneducated. And the issue is more acute for the poor than the well-off.

Second, America is witnessing the emergence of an underclass without parallel in our own personal experience. The situation is described in the quote by Daniel Patrick

Moynihan that opens this chapter. It is noteworthy that the quote was written in 1965 for an article in the Jesuit journal *America*. Not only was Moynihan right when he wrote these tragically prophetic words, he was also right when he said, "It is not a racial issue; it is a class issue."

Violence compounds the problem of poverty. As Fred Heckinger notes in his recent Carnegie study, *Fateful Choices:*

- At one inner-city clinic, 24 percent of the teenagers reported having seen a murder, while 72 percent knew someone who had been shot.

- Every 36 minutes a child is killed or injured by a gun, adding up to more than 14,000 children a year.

- In 1987, 338,000 students across the nation carried a handgun to school at least once during the year. Roughly eight times as many carried a knife.

There are powerful comparisons to America's situation, both historic and contemporary. Both are unsettling. One historic comparison is the poor of urbanizing and industrializing England of the late eighteenth and nineteenth centuries. The closest thing to a modern comparison is the teeming cities of the Third World, swelling with the mass migration of illiterate, rural poor as they seek a better life in an urban setting. The parallels with modern America are obvious and alarming.

A corollary problem, as Moynihan pointed out, is the dissolution of the family, not just in the underclass, but in society as a whole.

Since 1960 we have seen a steady increase in the rate of divorce, resulting in children being raised in one-parent families. In 1960, the divorce rate was one in four; in 1990 it was one in two. Furthermore, in 1960, only 4.2 percent of children lived with a never-married parent; by 1990, it had risen to 30.6 percent. In 1988 (the most recent year for which such statistics are available), 26 percent of all newborn babies were born to unmarried women, but in 1960 it was 5.3 percent. More people are alone, and more children are being raised by single parents. Running parallel to the collapse of the immediate family has been an increase in drug abuse, incarceration, and violent crime.

Children of the underclass and of broken homes are clearly at risk, and schools are increasingly being asked to take on roles outside of their traditional sphere, to fill in the gap where parents and community are falling down. Before examining the effect of these developments on education, let us look at the role of parents in their children's education, and how schools can connect with families to help them carry out this role.

School/Family Interaction: The Parents' Role in Education

How should the school connect with families to help them reinforce their children's education? Next Century Schools provide concrete examples of what can be done and how to do it.

First, schools should establish and promulgate standards for school readiness. Schools should let parents and the community at large know what the fundamentals of school readiness are, from prenatal health care to reading to young children. Fortunately, few parents deliberately choose to be poor parents; most poor parenting is due to inadequate knowledge, a problem schools can help remedy. The most obvious step is to assemble information on good child-rearing practices and then to ensure that this information reaches parents. At Morgan County Elementary School in Madison, Georgia, for example, a cadre of parent volunteers has been organized to visit the homes of parents with pre-schoolers, to provide information about school readiness, and the importance of reading, nutrition, and health care. Similar programs have been developed at a number of other Next Century Schools. As one principal commented, "We consider these to be our children as soon as they are born."

Not surprisingly, parent/school contacts are most frequent and intense at the elementary school level; they begin to fade and even disappear at the middle school and high school level. Establishing contact with new parents, long before school begins, is a way for the school district to show both that it cares and that parents have some responsibility to prepare their youngsters for school. A logical outgrowth of such contacts is the creation of "pre-school PTAs," a device to provide new parents with a forum for discussing issues of intellectual and physical development and school readiness. In addition to simple printed matter, a parent-outreach program, particularly in communities with disadvantaged or poor parents, can be a powerful tool to encourage school readiness. Equally useful is an active parenting-education program, run in the school, to provide parents with information about preparing their children for school.

School readiness, usually thought of in terms of pre-school, is actually a continuing process. There is one constant, but the specifics change. The constant is that parents should try to create an environment in which there is a genuine commitment to learning. Not surprisingly, families that value learning and academic achievement have children that usually do significantly better than average. There are other constants which are variations on the theme of commitment to learning. TV viewing must be regulated and monitored; science and nature specials, the news (viewed regularly), and educational programming generally are superior to pure entertainment. Even dinner table conversation seems to help. Indeed, available research indicates that so long as there is a dinner table around which family members talk, the downside of TV viewing is moderated. Even kids who watch several hours a day are less negatively affected if the family shares ideas and talks to each other around regularly scheduled meals—with the TV turned off!

Reading should be a prized family activity. Who has ever met a normal child who didn't enjoy being read to at an early age? Reading aloud, even for as few as fifteen minutes a day, is one of the most powerful tools known to build school readiness in young kids, and it can continue into the later years. Once a child has learned to read, encouraging and rewarding silent reading—through conversation and moral support—is enormously important.

Glenwood Elementary in Chapel Hill, North Carolina, has taken reading to children a step further, by using low technology and a lot of imagination. Kids everywhere love Dr. Seuss stories, and during a parent-student activity program, preschoolers and their parents are served "green eggs and ham," a Seuss favorite. To add to the fun—and the learning—the kids are encouraged to use a "zap" camera, to take pictures of themselves and their parents *and* of the green eggs and ham, all of which are then shown on a TV monitor. This is a simple introduction to technology, but for preschoolers it is the first time they have seen themselves or their parents on television. And it reinforces the students' and parents' interest in reading.

Another constant that is very important is a student's attitude toward school. Home is where that attitude is first shaped, and then reinforced. Parents have a responsibility to instill two ideas about school. First, kids should understand that school is a welcoming and friendly place; parents can demonstrate that they believe this to be true by being active in the life of the school: joining the PTA or PTO, pitching in as a volunteer, talking to the principal and to their youngster's teachers, current or prospective, and talking to other parents. Second, kids must understand that school is a place where "kids go to work"; school is their "work," and must be performed just as parents must perform their work, both at home and in the workplace for pay. School is not "camp," though on occasion it is as much fun; school is not babysitting, though it performs a custodial function. It is more than a place to socialize, though students properly socialize in school just as workers do in the workplace. School is a place to learn, to work hard, and to prepare for the world beyond school. There is not school and then something else called "the real world," or "life"; school *is* the real world, school *is* life. The sooner kids understand this, the better.

The New Role of Schools in Modern Society: Social Service Provider

What about the special case of kids who are at risk? It would be difficult to exaggerate how serious the problem is perceived to be by teachers and principals. One of the most striking aspects of the Next Century Schools competition is the near unanimity expressed by thousands of applicants about the dreadful state of the American family. No one is closer to the problem than they, no one cares more, and no one bears a larger share of the burden.

Fully 80 percent of the proposals submitted to the Foundation directly addressed the difficulty schools face today as a consequence of the dissolution of the family. Indeed, so severe is the problem that a number of proposals grimly observed that they were no longer dealing with one-parent families, but no-parent families, in which children had been abandoned altogether.

Clearly, a dangerous social divide is opening in America. The underclass that is emerging, dangerous both to itself and to the larger society, brings with it the problems of poverty, homelessness, abandonment, drugs, disease, violence, and teenage pregnancy. Individually, these problems are not new. What is new is their apparent permanence and severity. Once, when problems like these surfaced in our farms and cities, we thought they were incidental and transitory. Optimists, at least, believed that most people could rise above their mean circumstances. America was, after all, the land of opportunity. Yet today the underclass appears to be stuck in a morass of despair, hopelessness, and antisocial behavior. If the underclass is stuck, we are stuck with it. We are all in it together.

What is the effect on our schools? As the family unit disintegrates, the society at large expects schools to play even greater roles; indeed, the society demands schools to become surrogate families: nurturer and disciplinarian, day-care center and teacher, counsellor and peace-keeper.

The most striking evidence is offered by the explosive growth of year-round schools in North Carolina, a direct offshoot of the Mooresville Next Century Schools program. As we noted earlier, Mooresville had a major selling task on its hands when the idea of year-round schools was first broached. As eloquent as Superintendent Sam Houston is, even he found the task daunting. Yet three years later, year-round schooling in North Carolina is booming, and Mooresville can barely accommodate the endless stream of visitors. What's at work? Schools have always "fit" into the larger set of social and economic realities of the real world. The agricultural calendar existed for a reason—it worked. It will soon yield to a year-round calendar for the same reason. As Mooresville demonstrates, there is a compelling need on the part of parents to have suitable, safe, and sensible care for their children when the 180-day school year is not in session. And the increase from no year-round schools in North Carolina when Mooresville began, to 85 today offers ample evidence that imitation is the sincerest form of flattery.

Evidence of this trend, of course, is not restricted to Next Century Schools. In Murphrysboro, Tennessee, for example, an inventive and indefatigable superintendent, John Hodge Jones, has created a national model for extending the school day and school year. With 4,000 students in his district, Jones now enrolls half in extended-day programs, including dozens of youngsters from adjoining counties who pay tuition to attend. The Murphrysboro program includes a rich variety of after-school activities, including age-group soccer, Kumon math, 4-H, instrumental music, dance, and scouting—all for a fee: $35 per week for the first child, with discounts for siblings. How does Murphrysboro do it? As home to Middle Tennessee State College, it has large numbers of competent and eager young people ready to work in the local schools. But that's only part of the story. The real story is leadership—on Jones's part—and a willingness to take risks. Chapter One, the federal government's most ambitious elementary and secondary school remedial program, is ordinarily offered during the day as a "pull-out" program, a practice of dubious academic value. Jones offers Chapter One after school, both to provide a "free" after-school activity for poor youngsters and to rationalize the pedagogy. As an after-school program, Chapter One children are no longer "pulled out" of regular classes for remedial work (which has the perverse effect of denying them the instructional time they would otherwise have with their regular teacher); neither do they bear the stigma with fellow students of being pull-out kids. Finally, an after-school setting permits more time on task for Chapter One kids, and it provides more space— normal, full-size classrooms—rather than the overflow space classes are stuck with for pull-out programs. Test results aren't in yet, but smart money has it that Jones's Chapter One experiment will produce higher test scores—and happier Chapter One families.

The increase of family instability and the rise of violent crime in our cities makes it imperative that we control crime in the streets and the schools before we do anything else. Homicide is now the leading cause of death among young adults in many American cities, and the source of violence by and against children is due to family breakdown. As Fred Heckinger notes, "Black male adolescents are five to six times as likely to die as a result of homicide as white males. Black girls are two to three times as likely to become victims as white girls." In fact, for the first time since the Second World War, life expectancy for blacks has actually fallen (due to crime and drugs) despite the advances made in medicine, technology, and nutrition. Much of the cause for such despairing news is the prevalence of broken homes.

What do these grim numbers have to do with education

and schooling? A good deal. That poverty and disorder remain with us in the midst of plenty is a source of profound discouragement and disappointment. Not long ago—when the Great Society was born in the early and mid-sixties— many thought that they could control and eventually eliminate poverty with social programs just as the Corps of Engineers controlled flooding with dams and levees. And the great flood of 1993 demonstrated that not even the Corps of Engineers can hold back a once-in-a-century flood. The same is true in our cities. We have learned that if there is a metaphor for poverty in the natural world, it is tornadoes and earthquakes, not flood control. With careful planning and good luck, we can ameliorate the worst effects, but we cannot "eliminate" them.

The persistence—even growth—of an underclass raises the most troubling questions about the efficacy of schooling. Traditionally, schooling has been the one way to get up and out of poverty and destitution. Yet it seems not to work for many Americans, particularly those mired in the ghettoes of our central cities. Indeed, many observers fear the problem is beyond the reach of conventional social policy.

In earlier eras, having no education was a sentence to a life of hard labor. Today, it is a sentence to a life of no labor, of indolence and, in too many cases, a life of crime. It is no accident that 62 percent of state prison inmates are high school drop-outs.

Schools must also deal with large numbers of immigrants. The big, brawling urban school systems of the late nineteenth and early twentieth centuries dealt with an extraordinarily varied urban rabble, the product of internal rural-to-urban migration as well as overseas immigration. There was nothing like it before in history, and may never be again. "Riff-raff," they were thought of—the drunken

Irish, the poverty-stricken Southern Italians, black share-croppers from the agricultural south, Jews from the ghettoes of Central and Eastern Europe; never has the nation witnessed a more spectacular movement of different people.

Tempting though it is to think that today's problems are unique, they differ only in degree from the era of our grandparents and great-grandparents, and the difference in degree is in our favor. Although it is not unusual to hear complaints that floods of immigrants are to blame for crises in schools today such as crowding and the variety of languages and cultures which do not seem to readily assimilate, immigration rates in the past have been much higher. For example, the years immediately preceding the First World War witnessed the greatest wave of foreigners arriving in the history of the United States. Although the number of immigrants has risen since then—in 1914 there were more than 1.2 million immigrants, contrasted to 1.5 million in 1990—immigration has actually fallen significantly relative to the total population. The population is much larger now than it was eighty years ago, numbering 93 million in 1910, and almost 250 million in 1990, and thus is better able to absorb newcomers.

Horace Mann's common school—the precursor of the modern school—was designed with that population in mind. Mann, a state legislator and the nation's first school commissioner, created public education as we know it today precisely to ameliorate these problems. He "sold" his ideas to the business and civic elites of nineteenth-century Massachusetts as a device to solve the social problems of the day. As a devout Unitarian (and supporter of prayer in the schools), Mann believed that public schools would be institutions of moral uplift as well. Education interested Mann both as a way to tame the savage beast and as a way to create a workforce for the emerging industrial revolution. Schools

210

would moderate class differences, socialize the immigrant, and provide a moral framework for all citizens.

The one broadly based social institution where the problems of the underclass come to the surface is schools. To be sure, the underclass surfaces in a myriad of social institutions—the criminal justice system, public housing, hospital emergency rooms, the welfare system. These, however, are only compartments, far removed from the day-to-day experience of most middle-class Americans. Indeed, the only middle-class Americans in regular contact with the underclass are the middle-class teachers, principals, and students who join them in school. It was once thought that enrolling the poor and dispossessed with their more fortunate colleagues would make a significant difference in their lives; unhappily, this has not been the case. Then it was thought that Head Start and Title One (now Chapter One) would make a critical difference; these programs help, but not enough. Moreover, putting an end to racial barriers and dismantling the last vestiges of officially sanctioned racial segregation was considered enough to improve the situation of the underclass—it has not been.

In many respects the most troubling question before the nation is the question of culture. What role does culture play in education? On the plus side of the ledger, we know that immigrant cultures that prize education—Northern Europeans, Jews, Asians, blacks from the Caribbean Islands—can extract a good education from the most ordinary schools. Through hard work, diligence, and application, individuals can become educated; students become educated in spite of poor schools, because they are supported both by parents and by a larger culture that values education.

A recent study highlighted in *Scientific American* makes the point powerfully. Children of Indo-Chinese boat people,

arriving with little or no English, little or no money, mysti-
fied, fascinated, and frightened by the hubbub of American
culture, rise to the occasion when they get to school. And
the school they get to is typically a troubled inner-city
school. These youngsters, carrying heavy baggage, never-
theless master English and become first-rate students. How
do they do it? Culture plays a large part; education is held in
high regard. But the word *culture* can obscure as much as it
reveals; by explaining everything it explains nothing. What
particulars in their background and their culture account for
their academic success? In part, it is parents who believe in
education and encourage and reward academic success.
Their belief is not abstract but practical; they are convinced
that a good education will improve the life chances of their
children. In addition, brothers, sisters, aunts, uncles, and
friends believe in education, and let youngsters know it. As
well, the boat children learn at an early age that education is
satisfying; they learn that school is interesting and enjoyable.
They take pleasure in solving problems, typically games, but
intellectual problems nonetheless.

Three other aspects of culture stand out in this study, all
confirmed by site visits and interviews. First, children in
larger families do better than those in smaller ones, a surprising finding in an American context (most education research in America shows that kids from smaller families do
better). What's going on in the refugee families? Older kids
are role models, mentors, and tutors. They help the younger
kids both by example and with practice. Second, more "egalitarian" families produce kids with higher test scores. By
"egalitarian" the researchers mean those families in which
household work and chores are fairly shared among the family members. Mother doesn't wait on Dad or the kids; everyone pitches in. Third, not only is TV viewing limited and

reading encouraged, the values of hard work, honesty, and high principles are regularly and continuously reinforced.

Culture, then, is not a disembodied idea—it is the sum total of attitudes, habits, and activities that make a difference in the lives of children. And while the Indo-Chinese refugees are an example of a culture that supports and encourages educational attainment, the American "culture of poverty," entrenched in the underclass, too often discourages it. But even though discussion of culture invites misunderstanding both about motives and about cause and effect, the subject is too important to ignore.

The most pernicious aspect of the culture of poverty is the way in which it devalues education. In some cases there is overt hostility to education: "Thinking white," Ogbu calls it. Author of an important study on low academic achievement among black youngsters, what he says has a bearing on youngsters in general, particularly kids from impoverished and disorganized backgrounds. Black or white, Hispanic or Anglo, there is a tendency among poor and dispossessed Americans to think that education is for someone else, that only the fortunate few benefit from it. As a consequence, it is disparaged. Most immigrants know better. Why is this issue so important? Because motivation lies at the heart of education. Schooling is not a matter of teachers pouring education into empty vessels called students. True, brilliant and gifted teachers can motivate many students who would otherwise not learn, but the burden of motivation cannot be placed solely on the teacher. In the final analysis, the student must be the worker, the student must be motivated to learn.

The problem of low academic achievement is not a problem restricted to the poor and disadvantaged; it is just more perilous for them to be poorly educated. But low levels of academic achievement are endemic in American society, and too few of our youngsters take education as seriously as they must if we are to succeed in the next century. The role of parents as educators, and of communities as bearers of culture, must be restored.

How are these things known? Studies and new reports are important, of course. They help inform us. A recent poll of 1,400 high school students, for example, commissioned by the National Association of Secondary School Principals and the Sylvan Learning Corporation, reports that students across the board give their parents low marks for parental support of education.

But there is an even more potent source of information. Among the nearly four thousand Next Century Schools proposals, one feature stood out: the conviction that America stands at a crossroads and that our schools are called upon to do two things that are new. The first is to educate large numbers of otherwise able youngsters who are profoundly disconnected from school; the second is to educate the new "class" of youngsters, the "underclass."

A critical feature in reaching both sets of youngsters is reaching their parents and engaging them. A parent is the child's first teacher, and supportive parents can be powerful school allies. Yet many of the parents the schools need to reach had unhappy experiences in school themselves, and are reluctant to return, even for their children. Indeed, in some circumstances, parents will actively tell their children that school is an unwelcome and unhappy place. Molholm Elementary in Lakewood, Colorado, is acutely aware of this problem, and has found an unusual remedy. With a high transiency rate in the community, many of the families live in motels or temporary housing. As a consequence, they are only too happy to use the school washer and dryer—donated

214

for the purpose by local business. Practical outreach of this kind can readily translate into longer term, more effective parent-school relationships. And once the parents are involved, they begin to give back to the schools by volunteering on field trips, helping a teacher move into a new space, or assisting on the playground.

Most schools are ill-equipped to meet this challenge. The teachers and principals who applied to Next Century Schools were not uttering a lament about the state of America so much as about the inability of schools, as they are currently organized and run, to deal with these problems. Many of the proposals showed a sophisticated understanding of the issue; the students are qualitatively different children who must become educated if they are to have any hope at all. If society is to have any hope, these children must become educated. We are all in the same boat.

But the schools can't blame their raw material. Too many adults do just that: They wring their hands and assert that these kids can't learn (or can't cope, or can't get it right). Nothing could be farther from the truth. These kids can learn; these kids must learn. Indeed, they do learn, but they learn lessons of survival and coping, skills that stand them in good stead on mean streets and in prison, but do little for them in the world of adult work and citizenship.

Schools are confronted with the need to perform a balancing act; on the one hand, they cannot let the education budget hemorrhage to care for children in dire need. Schools are not and cannot become surrogate families. But they cannot ignore acute need either. John Murphy, when he was Superintendent of Prince George's County, Maryland, schools told a heart-wrenching story about how an elementary school child would beg to remain in school for the night, to avoid the fear, confusion, and danger he encountered at home in the projects. It is a powerful story, both literally and as a metaphor. School should be an oasis, one of calm and safety, and children in need must get access to help.

What can the schools do? Now Superintendent of Charlotte-Mecklenburg schools, Murphy is developing an approach that will soon be a national model. First and foremost, the district refuses to lose sight of its educational mission; however, it will assume one new function: *children's services broker and advocate.*

And what will the district do? First, the superintendent and the school board will turn to the larger community to address the needs of children in Mecklenburg county. They will propose that the full panoply of existing services be catalogued and made available to the community, ranging from child-protection services to United Way programs, from probation services to day-care services. And by children's services they mean not just public-sector activities, but private and not-for-profit as well. Second, they will orchestrate the creation of a child-services inventory, a descriptive and analytic look at what the children of Mecklenburg County need.

Murphy has turned to the community to help build support for private-sector involvement at the most basic and pressing level. Meeting with the Charlotte Interfaith Council—the leaders of Charlotte's churches and synagogues—Murphy asked them to assume responsibility for developing a network of day-care services across the county. Houses of worship are ideally suited to day care, because of their geographic distribution throughout the community and their physical capacity. Typically they have the space, the kitchen and bathroom facilities, and the administrative and managerial know-how to set up and run effective day-care operations. And they have the motivation and the support of members of their institutions. Perhaps most important, they

216

can infuse day care in these settings with educational values that stress school readiness.

Murphy believes that it is time to involve churches, synagogues, and mosques in the work of schools. He is convinced that the wall of separation between church and state cannot be used as a device to postpone or avoid helping children in need; religious institutions, without coming under state control or improperly influencing the state, should be partners in the process as well. Once such programs are in place, the public schools can play a supportive role; they can use day-care centers as outreach opportunities, both for meetings with prospective public school parents and as settings for parenting education.

What other kinds of things might the schools do to address at least some of the problems? Keeping in mind that the school's first obligation is to educate, they can cast their educational net wider to include parents. This theme runs through countless Next Century Schools grant requests, and is central to a number of Next Century School awards. The Park View School in Chapel Hill, North Carolina, for example, has placed parent education at the center of its program to increase student performance. Parent outreach, combined with a carefully thought-out program of parent education, increases the likelihood of greater parental involvement with their children's education.

A comment heard again and again in Next Century Schools applications and programs is that parents are well intentioned, even eager to participate, but don't understand how or what they might do to become involved in their child's education. Most parents of this kind were themselves ignored as children—either by commission or omission. They did not have the kind of experiences middle-class families take for granted. There were no books or magazines in the home; no caring adult to read out loud, answer questions, or reward intellectual curiosity; and television was the ubiquitous baby-sitter. Such lack of academic support at home too often translates into academic failure in school, which in turn leads to fear of, or worse yet, contempt for, education.

As we have noted previously, one of the most potent and effective things a school can do to increase parental involvement, both with the school and with individual children, is to put in place an effective parent-outreach program. Ortega Elementary, a Next Century School in Austin, Texas, has such a program in place. As a special-emphasis school because of the high incidence of poverty in the surrounding community, Ortega receives special funding from the Austin School Board for a parent-outreach counselor. The need is great.

An unprepossessing building in a decaying neighborhood, Ortega not only needs parental involvement educationally, but needs parental involvement to keep the wolves at bay. The most striking visual feature of the neighborhood is junked cars on blocks, long ago abandoned. Opposite the school's back door is an open-air drug market. The teachers' parking lot, which is surrounded by a high chain-link fence, has been the scene of three car thefts in broad daylight in the last year. Five computers and peripherals—part of the NCS award—were stolen in the first six months of the original NCS grant. And so common is theft from poor schools in Austin that the school district is now "self-insured," a euphemism for no insurance and no replacement.

As difficult as the environment around Ortega is, once inside the building the student enters another world—one that is spotlessly clean, brightly decorated, and full of parent volunteers, men and women there to make Ortega a better place. They provide support for instruction and extracurricular activities, oversee fund-raisers, and participate in parent education and outreach programs.

The key to Ortega's outreach, however, is a paid home-liaison person, an Ortega parent who deals with all the day-to-day problems of a school in a troubled neighborhood. When a child fails to report to school in the morning, the home is called; if there is no answer, or an unsatisfactory or unconvincing answer, the home-liaison person appears at the front door. No excuses. If the child is ill, homework assignments are coordinated; if the child is goofing off, it's off to school. No excuses.

Many good ideas for parental involvement in schools that were part of NCS grant applications could not be funded by the Foundation. A high school in McNairy, Tennessee, that was a 1992 Finalist, though not a winner, proposed contracts between parents and the school that include an agreement to limit students' TV viewing. Murry Bergtraum, the nation's premier high school of office and secretarial arts, located in the heart of New York's Wall Street area, is in the process of forming an "emeritus corps," former teachers who will maintain an association with the school and help enlarge its parent-outreach program.

Business can play a strong role in encouraging closer links between schools and parents. Obvious strategies include such things as broadening day-care options and encouraging employees to play a more active role in the life of schools. Increasing options for day care may include a wide range of activities, depending on the size and scale of the employer as well as the employer's location and facilities.

One option, pioneered by Honeywell in Minnesota, under the leadership of CEO Jim Renier, is to provide day care on a fee basis on the premises. Honeywell has the financial and physical resources to launch such a program; smaller employers may find that they can include a day-care subsidy as part of the menu of employee benefits—an employee may choose a day-care benefit rather than health care, a benefit that may already be available through a spouse's employer.

At the day-to-day level of business and school operations, employers, including those that employ large numbers of hourly workers, can devise systems of release time or flex scheduling to permit parents to attend parent/school meetings or conferences. They can also offer "parenting programs" as part of employee education and training.

At the policy level, business can encourage able employees to run for school boards and not penalize those who serve. Release or flex time should be offered for board members as well as parents, and community service contributions should reflect favorably on an employee's career.

One of the most interesting innovations of the past decade has been the creation, on business sites, of school programs, either full- or part-time, for kids of all ages. *Cities in Schools,* the brainchild of one-time street minister Bill Milliken, has enjoyed unprecedented success across the country. Most notable is a downtown school in Atlanta housed on the top floor of Rich's Department Store. For many Rich's employees this presents an opportunity to volunteer; the kids in the program, many of whom are from the projects where three generations of unemployment is the norm, get to see a rare sight: Adults gainfully employed, who like their work, and communicate their enthusiasm to the students.

The Foundation has also played a pioneering role in a similar endeavor. The Downtown School in Winston-Salem, North Carolina, is housed in a former public market, near a major corporate complex. First claim on the school is enjoyed by the children of workers, who as a condition of enrollment must volunteer at least one hour a week. Parents are able to spend more time with their youngsters, whether volunteering or taking lunch hours at the school. The logic of work-based assignment schools is apparent. Particularly as more and more mothers enter the workforce, closer ties between school and the workplace become ever more important.

How Schools Can Reinforce Parents and Communities

This chapter has looked at how schools can reach out to parents and communities and engage them in their children's education, and also at how parents and communities can reinforce, or fail to reinforce, schools. This interaction is a two-way street. There are also certain ways in which schools can reinforce families and communities, and make a difference in the everyday lives of children. We know, for example, that feeding programs make a difference in the lives of hungry children, just as health screening and inoculations are important. Schools can also make a difference in simple ways, offering some small comfort to children by providing a warm, well-lighted place away from the cares and concerns of the street, and, most important, some measure of sensitive custodial care.

Indeed, it is in this area that Next Century Schools offer the most compelling examples of school/family and community reinforcement. The most important example is the extended-day and extended-year concept, most fully developed in Mooresville, North Carolina. In Park View Elementary, the extended day and year serve both academic and social purposes. Park View not only provides a safe and wholesome environment, it provides continuing academic development and enrichment. This Next Century School is a model for the nation, and has attracted national attention, because it meets community needs so successfully. For children who need remediation or additional work to keep abreast of the class, an intersession is offered; so too there are intersessions for kids who want to range ahead in the curriculum. Then there is an intersession that is straight child care, but it too is enriched; it is not just baby-sitting. It is child care with content, the best kind.

Schools can also reinforce parents and community by requiring that their students perform school and community service. Such service is more than an additional source of energy and effort; it is a powerful device to bind the school community together. The options for community service are almost limitless: working in day-care centers, old peoples' homes, hospitals, and rehabilitation centers, other schools— the list goes on. And whatever kids do in the way of service is a form of community connection. Done willingly and well, community service sends an unequivocal message that students care. They care enough to pitch in and help. And the help is real. It makes the community a better place. But more important, it makes the student a better person. It is a form of character development.

The importance of the invisible curriculum, the nonacademic areas of student development, would be hard to overemphasize. Once upon a time schools were not embarrassed about their responsibility to form character. Schools should reclaim this legacy, and work directly on character formation. However, character is not formed by lectures and exhortations; character is formed by example and practice. As Aristotle observed, men become virtuous by behaving virtuously. Practice makes perfect.

To this end, school and community service are the keys

to character formation. The North Carolina School of Science and Mathematics requires school and community service as a condition of graduation, but is highly flexible in making this demand on students. As a boarding school, opportunities for community service in the area near the school are occasionally limited, and students are permitted—even encouraged—to meet their community service obligation in their hometowns.

School and community service are essential to the intellectual and moral development of students. As every American knows, if we are charged by court of law, we all have a right to a trial by a jury of our peers. So too we have an obligation to serve on a jury if called. School should be no different. Just as we enjoy the benefits conferred by school, students should be prepared to return the favor and participate in support activities for the school itself. No task should be considered off limits, from leaf-raking to clerical work in the office. But the most important role a student can play in school is as a tutor, mentor, and role model for other students.

All of this reinforces what should be an unself-conscious commitment on the part of schools to an old-fashioned idea: character formation. Character formation has been a major responsibility of schools. Education has never existed in a vacuum. It has a purpose: Make the world a better place by making students better people. At no time in our history has this issue been more important. Watching Los Angeles burn for the second time in thirty years should have reminded us all that schools are an important forum for creating and maintaining civic virtue. Not a single school in Los Angeles was touched by vandals or arsonists. Not one! While schools cannot solve the problems of race and social class, they are the public sector's first line of defense in dealing with the questions of social justice and humane values.

The social pathology highlighted by the Los Angeles riots is all the worse because it is a self-inflicted wound. America's troubled communities are the product of the most difficult and distressing social pathology, a form of personal and social self-abuse—drugs, AIDS, violence, crime, homicide, and the abandonment of wives by husbands and of children by parents as grandparents are called upon to raise grandchildren.

So long as such events are not the norm, the social fabric can stretch and accommodate. But at some point a critical mass is reached, and deviant behavior becomes the new norm, not just because it is widespread but because it becomes accepted behavior. The occasional illegitimate birth becomes commonplace; the few fathers who abandon their wives and children become a rash of abandonment and the next generation is left with no positive role model. Worse yet, the next generation accepts these changes as normal.

There has been much talk about a National Children's Policy, but it would be surprising if there is sufficient knowledge (let alone wisdom) at the national level to do more than talk about such a policy now or in the near future. There are, of course, things that could and should be done at the national level. For example, tax policy could be rationalized and the allowance for dependent children could be greatly increased to keep up with inflation. Welfare could be changed to "workfare." With more than two-thirds of mothers with children now working, the notion that welfare mothers should be given the resources to remain home with their children is, at best, quaint. Indeed, "not working" may be the most serious problem welfare presents. Welfare's original purpose was to ameliorate the problem of not working, but its effect has been to enable not working to become a semi-permanent state. The problem is more acute than producing or not producing income; not working produces negative values and attitudes, leading people to believe that effort and income are not connected, that enterprise, diligence, and high standards are of no consequence.

But these national remedies are long-term and far removed from the day-to-day activities of schools. At the local level, there is every reason to think that conversations about these issues could bear fruit. Communities like Charlotte-Mecklenburg, and others across the nation, can create children's boards both to begin the discussion and to give it shape and focus.

The Ultimate Role of Parents and Community: Financial Support

The real power of parent and community involvement is that they will then be more motivated to provide the support schools need to be effective. Schools must let the community and parents know what is expected of them, both to get young children ready to begin school and to get older youngsters to succeed in school. The range of needs is great in any community, from day care to jobs for needy high school students. So too is the range of possible responses.

Schools must also let the community know what resources they need, and why. Who has not heard the lament that schools today are expected to be all things to all people? They are surrogate parents, part-time policemen, counselors and social workers, nurses and psychologists, fast-food emporia and health clubs all rolled into one. It is hard to imagine schools meeting any of these obligations well, let alone all of them. But if it is true that schools are now expected to serve all these masters, then they must strike out in one new direction that few have thought about yet. They must design and put in place a new budgeting system, one that displays what they really do.

It is easy to blame the Congress, the state legislature, the board of county commissioners, city hall—whomever—for the school's woes. But the schools are partly responsible. They have accepted more and more responsibility with only weak protests. In part this is true because schools, like the rest of us, saw the rough justice, if not the wisdom, in assigning more tasks to them that had to do with children. Alone among our social institutions, schools deal with everyone from the age of first grade to the end of compulsory attendance; it makes administrative sense for schools to screen for childhood diseases, feed the poor, and minister to the confused. But such tasks are nothing if not expensive.

Traditionally, instructional and noninstructional costs defined the school budget, just as capital and noncapital expenditures define most budgets. Many schools now distinguish between capital and noncapital expenditures; many schools also display an instructional and noninstructional budget separately; some schools even display indirect costs and overhead separately.

But today's school budgets should also display the cost of activities that fall wholly outside the school's academic mission. It is the rare school that does this. Yet only in this way will schools be able to reclaim their academic mission. Schools that are able to cost out the price of custodial care, feeding, counseling, busing, and the like are schools that will be able to make a claim on the community for greater resources. And that, in the final analysis, is what community support is all about.

CHAPTER 9

Productivity
in Schools

*Pedants sneer at an education which is useful. But if
education is not useful, what is it? Is it a talent to be
hidden away in a napkin? Of course education should
be useful, whatever your aim in life. It was useful to
Saint Augustine and it was useful to Napoleon. It is
useful because understanding is useful.*

—Alfred North Whitehead,
The Aims of Education

America's schools face a productivity crisis; they are expensive, inefficient, and antiquated. We know what they cost, but not the value of what they produce. Public schools are measured by what society spends on them, not by what they give back. Until society measures the value of education, it is impossible to make informed judgments about how much we *should* spend on education.

This reasoning runs counter to what most educators and many parents think the problem is: lack of money. Total spending on education in America is without equal in the world. Public schools receive generous public support from all sources. The nation invested more than $230 billion in public elementary and secondary schools in 1991. And parents dipped into their own pockets for $25 billion for private school tuitions. That's a lot of money, even by Washington standards. Only health care commands more. More important, however, is one fact: Expenditures for public education increased in the decade of the eighties by 34 percent (in real dollars), yet the only output measures available were test scores, which were, by and large, static. Indeed, in the eighties there was only one bit of good news on the education productivity front: Test scores of black students climbed slowly but steadily.

At an anecdotal level, we are all familiar with our school's output shortfalls: students who cannot and do not learn, unacceptably high drop-out rates, spiraling costs, reluctant and rebellious taxpayers, and frustrated teachers and administrators. We are also familiar with input problems. The nation's poorest schools suffer an array of problems: leaking roofs, inadequate supplies, old and irrelevant textbooks, no computers (or castoffs that no one else has a use for), demoralized faculties, and unsupportive parents.

What we lack is a convincing way to relate inputs to outputs. What difference does a dollar more, or a dollar less, make? There is no end of educated guesses, but no matter what problems schools confront, such as increasing or declining enrollments, English as a second language, teaching foreign languages, educating the handicapped, the gifted and talented, or the poor and dispossessed, most educators assert that more money is the answer.

Undoubtedly, more money would be welcome. But the issue is not what we would like to spend, but what society is prepared to pay for a service called "education." Indeed, the issue is not even what society can afford. As a wealthy country we can afford pretty much what we like. But no matter how rich America is or becomes, the question will remain: *How much of our wealth are we prepared to devote to education?* This question cannot be answered sensibly until we know with some confidence what additional money will buy in the way of increased output. The hard fact is that education competes for resources, and its claim is only as strong as its payoff.

Competition for scarce resources may sound harsh to educators, but it is a reality. Education not only competes with health, welfare, recreation, transportation, day care, and other social services, but education even competes with education—public elementary and secondary education compete with public higher education, job training, and graduate and professional schools. Each of these claimants for public funds has a perfectly good case to make; the nation needs researchers, doctors, and lawyers as well as teachers and businesspeople. The nation needs nurses and firemen, police officers and prison guards, librarians and retail clerks, actors and cameramen, toll-takers and heavy-equipment operators, as well as carpenters and plumbers. Not surprisingly, each of these groups would like to have more for itself, even if that means less for some other worthy purpose.

Public education is no exception. Who has not heard supporters of the schools assert that their problems are budgetary? Give schools more money and their problems can be corrected. Certainly, there is truth in all these claims and lamentations; in almost all endeavors, more money is preferred to less.

But money is only part of the story. Better rich and smart. Unfortunately, schools are not organized to work "smart"; it is not called mass education for nothing. Schools teach by brute force; they are based on an explicit factory model, with the teacher as the worker and the student as the product. Mass production is the objective. If all kids were the same, and if society expected and wanted identical outcomes, it might be possible to mass-produce education. Indeed, the Japanese come close to doing it that way: large classes, demanding teachers, a national curriculum, and national tests, together with extraordinarily hard-working students, produce powerful results. It is the educational equivalent of the Ford Motor Company River Rouge Plant of the 1950s.

We have done much the same thing for more than a century; we have treated the education of large numbers of youngsters as a mass-production challenge. But unlike Japan, which graduates 96 percent of its eighteen-year-olds, we have never reached even three-quarters of our kids. We graduate less than 75 percent of each age group. Our mass education was and is characterized by very high failure and drop-out rates. And as Al Shanker wryly notes, if one-quarter of your product falls off the assembly line, and another quarter doesn't work when it reaches the end of the line, you don't correct the problem by running the assembly line faster and longer. We need a new and different metaphor for schooling, one that addresses productivity directly.

What is productivity? It is an unfamiliar and uncongenial concept for most educators. For many people, combining the two terms—education and productivity—conjures up images of green-eye-shaded analysts looking for a school's "bottom line," and subverting the very purpose education is meant to serve. Obviously, there are limitations to economic analysis of schools; schools are not factories or even businesses. But schools are still supposed to take in children when they are young, and turn them into something they would not otherwise become. And that process takes time and money; and some schools are better at it than others.

Our task is to retain a clear sense of schooling's humane and liberal purposes, and to subject the process to clear-eyed and unromantic scrutiny. We must measure what we can; we must deal with the issue of educational productivity in an accurate and effective manner. First, everyone agrees that schools have both inputs and outputs. Productivity simply refers to the relationship, or ratio, between them. The relationship between the two is what is uncertain. The factors of production—time, money, physical plant, and the cost of capital—are inputs, just like a worker with a tool and a bench who makes something, or a person who sells an idea. Outputs are the goods or services produced: an automobile, a TV set, a hamburger, a medical diagnosis, an equation mastered, or a skill acquired.

Typically, schools emphasize inputs and what goes into a school, money in particular. Only rarely is an attempt made to connect inputs and outputs. This failure has serious consequences, because schools without productivity measures are unable to demonstrate how additional inputs will make a difference, how they will improve education. Without a clear sense of what it takes to produce desired outputs, we are asked to take schools on faith, a public-policy approach that invites, if it does not guarantee, skepticism.

In the private sector, by way of contrast, as the ratio between outputs and inputs rises, productivity increases. And increased productivity boosts wealth, both personal and social. The classic examples are drawn from the industrial and agricultural revolutions. Two hundred years ago, straight pins for sewing were made by hand, one at a time. One pin-maker could produce a few dozen pins a day. Modern, high-speed pin-making machines produce thousands of pins an hour. The productivity increase is measured by calculating the cost of production and the value of sales.

Note that two things happen; the pin-maker not only makes more pins but more money, and the pin-purchaser gets more pins for the pound. Productivity increases benefits for both the buyer and seller. And they are good for the economy as a whole because more wealth is created.

This wealth provides capital to invest in new activities and additional capacity. The nation as a whole is able to invest $230 billion per year in education because the resource base is so vast. But the resource base is vast because of the

233

way and the extent to which we use technology to increase output. As Joel Mokyr, author of *Lever of Riches,* points out, contrary to popular opinion, "there is a free lunch." It is called "technology" because it increases outputs for a given level of inputs. We get more for the same effort.

The most famous example of substantial productivity increases in the modern era was Henry Ford's perfection of the assembly line, which made it possible to mass-produce automobiles of high quality at a reasonable price. What was the real meaning of the assembly line? It was a triumph of "dumbing down" work, making it so simple and repetitive that even the simplest worker could do it so long as he had deft hands, a strong back, and a willing attitude. For assembly lines to operate, work must be organized so skillfully that virtually no human judgments have to be made to bring the product to completion.

The sad truth is that schools are not organized to be either productive or efficient, even by assembly-line standards, and certainly not by the standards of modern, high-performance organizations. Indeed, looking at them leaves one inescapable conclusion: Schools are organized to be inefficient. Grossly inefficient. Schools are low-tech, labor-intensive organizations with poorly articulated goals, low standards, and weak to nonexistent measures of performance. If someone—as in a case study done by a business school, for example—set out to design as inefficient an organization as could be conceived, it would be a modern public school.

Consider three factors: labor, plant and equipment, and materials.

Look at labor in a free economy. All successful enterprises use financial incentives and rewards (as well as disincentives and penalties) to encourage and recognize desirable

234

behavior. The reason is not simple altruism on the part of managers. Better employees are worth more, and produce more that is of value. To be precise, they earn more for the firm; they add more value than their compensation. The employer is not doing the employee a favor by offering higher wages for higher performance; rather, he is doing himself a favor because the firm enjoys greater profitability.

Why don't schools pay for performance as the rest of the economy does? Everyone in the building knows who the best teachers are; there's no real mystery there. Originally, schools didn't pay for performance because of blind adherence to the idea that all teachers did the same thing in the same way. The analogue was the assembly-line worker. Schools do not pay for performance today because they don't know how to measure it. The only exception in public education is football coaches, who frequently are paid more if they have winning seasons.

In the service economy, plant means more than the physical setting where work occurs; it includes the infrastructure of wire, fiber optics, and satellites that make the modern workplace possible. It is the technology the worker plugs into, the networks of data, and the information and communication the worker deals with. Much of the most important physical plant and equipment the modern worker uses is owned by someone else—the phone or satellite company, for example—and the worker rents time on the system.

The reservations clerk for an international airline is a perfect example; he or she works at a public counter in front of a computer terminal that puts him or her into contact with the whole world of travel and travelers. Without question, the contemporary public school is the lowest tech large-scale activity in the whole economy. The modern public school looks more like the schools of the early nineteenth century than the high-tech firm of the present.

The analogue in a school setting is the library with inter-active computers, or networked computers in the school it-self. Piscataquis High School in Guilford, Maine, is tied into a satellite dish both to receive commercial programs that are of special interest and utility, and for a distance-learning hook-up with the University of Maine. Situated in the Appa-lachian highlands of western Maine, Piscataquis High is in a county the size of Delaware, yet the county is so remote that there is not even a movie theater. Distance-learning in this setting means that accelerated students can take college-level calculus by TV hook-up with a professor of mathemat-ics; instead of being overcome by boredom or frustration, distance-learning students can stretch their intellectual hori-zons.

The idea of distance-learning is an old one in remote areas, but only now are schools thinking about it in produc-tivity terms. The North Carolina School of Science and Mathematics' NCS program is designed to find out if young-sters learn as well and as completely by using distance-learning as those students in conventional classrooms.

What are the materials of the service economy? Ideas. Books. Computer software. Networks. Knowledge. Although schools are expected to deal with ideas, by and large they do so very poorly. Some students deal with abstract ideas and "linear learning" very well; according to some estimates, perhaps a quarter of all students learn well this way. Most book readers, analysts, and people who manipulate symbols for a living learn this way. Didactic lectures, chalk talks, self-directed study, and homework are the hallmarks of this kind of learning. It is also what most teachers and administrators are most familiar with.

That is why until the mid-twentieth century most American education was "school-centered"; students were expected to accommodate themselves to the school—or else. The student did what the school asked, or simply left. If only a quarter of all learners fit well into this approach, it is no wonder the drop-out rate is high. For at least the last thirty years, many educators have recognized this problem, and have moved in the other direction. Schools have become "student-centered." Today's schools are expected to accommodate themselves to their students. No demands on students. Let them learn at their own pace, in their own way.

Anything goes; instead of ruthless adherence to discipline, which characterized the "school-centered" activities of an earlier era, the "student-centered" school lets kids get by. Al Shanker suggests, imagine a workplace in which no demands are made on workers, no standards are set, and none are met. Yet workers get paid whether they work or not, and whether the job is well done or not. Workers even get paid if they don't show up for work. What would happen? You'd get exactly what you would expect in the workplace. It should be no surprise if this sounds like a modern public school. Drop-outs? The schools are supposed to design programs to retain them. Low test scores? The schools are supposed to design programs to remedy this problem. Expect students to work on their own? Rarely.

Clearly, both the "student-centered" and "school-centered" approaches are inappropriate. No company could stay in business today if it adopted either extreme. But there is today, in business and in other high-performance organizations, a science of management. We now understand in large measure how to manage our most important resource: people. Not manipulate, but manage. We do so by understanding what their needs, interests, and capacities are. Peter

Drucker, for example, goes so far as to say that there are not bad workers, only workers out of place. If managers hired them in the first place, it is up to managers to identify and assign them work they can do. Strong medicine, but it has direct implications for the schools.

There is a middle ground, one being assiduously developed by Next Century Schools. Relying heavily upon computers, the school of the next century can establish high and rigorous standards for all and at the same time tailor offerings to fit the needs of each student. Sir Francis Drake High School in Marin, California, is a Next Century School with a special corporate partner: Autodesk. As developers and marketers of some of the most sophisticated CAD-CAM software in the world, Autodesk has been quick to see extraordinary possibilities for its technical competency in education.

Building CAD-CAM expertise into drawing software, Autodesk produces *Animator* and *Animator Pro,* programs that turn students into cartoonists and illustrators. Serious science has a home at Sir Francis Drake as well thanks to Autodesk, which has developed a fascinating and brilliant program called *Chaos.* Named after and designed to work with James Glieck's summarized material engaging the study of random events, *Chaos* puts complex ideas into visible form. For most adults, to whom computers are alien machines, a walk through a school like Sir Francis Drake is a true eye-opener. Students are as at home with computers as they are with video games, and they work with programs like *Animator Pro* and *Chaos* with the ease of seasoned professionals. When using *Animator Pro,* a student can design, lay out, adjust, and edit, and then print-out a "tide pool." When using *Chaos,* a student can begin to trace and understand the behavior of random movement: the movements of particles suspended in liquid or of molecules in a plasma.

Programs like this put the question of technology in a different perspective. Consider the observation of Patricia Graham, former Harvard Graduate School of Education Dean (and NCS Advisory Board member). As an education historian, Graham notes that in the nineteenth century and most of the twentieth century, schools "held the pedagogy constant and let the results vary." Today, we must have schools with high and rigorous standards and results. That means in the future we will have to "vary the pedagogy to get uniform, high results." To put it in economic terms, it is a question of service-sector productivity.

To understand how to improve productivity, schools must first clearly understand what their purpose is. What value do they add? What do they do with students to make them better or smarter people? How are students changed and improved by attending school? And how can schools do a better job? If schools fail to come to terms with their purposes it is no wonder that they cannot establish processes and procedures that make sense. It is equally no wonder that the public becomes skeptical, particularly about requests for more money.

Once schools understand their purpose, they will understand more clearly who their clients and workers are. Their clients are the larger society: Society pays the bills and wants results. Schools' workers are not the teachers, though they do work hard. Their workers must be the students. Teachers must become managers of instruction. That is where the biggest productivity gains will occur.

There is nothing wrong with the teachers; they have the knowledge. And there is nothing wrong with kids' basic intelligence. The problem is the system. Teachers do not "transfer" knowledge to unresponsive pupils by pounding it into them; pupils must work to acquire it. But this does not mean that schools should return to the insensitive behavior of an earlier era any more than business should return to sweatshops. Cracking the whip is not the way to get high performance out of workers; making them part of the team is. High expectations, which they share and internalize, produces high performance—which is, in turn, rewarded. Again, the reward to a worker is not a prize, it is earned— the old-fashioned way. This is true with a vengeance of the forty-two schools that make up the national network of Next Century Schools. They didn't receive a prize from the RJR Nabisco Foundation; they didn't win the education lottery. They went head-to-head with four thousand other schools in a rigorous competition and *earned* their awards.

One of the major challenges all schools face is to increase productivity, despite the anxieties of many teachers. Confronted with the prospect of a new technology, workers are frequently afraid that machines will replace people, that an emphasis on productivity will make the workplace inhospitable and consumed with concerns about the bottom line. The history of productivity increases has been uneven at times, but the overall picture has been one of improvement. The unevenness has been a function of uncertain implementation. Think of the mature assembly line; first viewed as a boon to workers (no longer were they working long hours in difficult conditions in fields and mines), the first assembly-line workers were protected from the elements and worked regular hours for regular pay. It was not long, however, before industrial observers noticed that assembly lines had their own problems. Long hours of simple, repetitive work were boring; it was difficult to maintain quality on long production runs. And so work teams were born, from Volvo in Sweden and Belgium and Honda in Japan and the U.S. to the new General Motors Saturn plants in the U.S.

Are there analogies in the world of education? First there are the historical breakthroughs that make modern mass education possible. What distinguishes modern education from that of the Middle Ages? Gutenberg's movable type, which was the beginning of modern printing, made the modern textbook and workbook possible. John Amos Comenius, the Czech educator, invented the modern textbook. He took education out of the study, where a single tutor worked with a handful of children, and made it possible for dozens of children to work with one teacher.

But it sowed the seeds of its own discontent. Interestingly, one of the themes that ran through countless NCS proposals was a thorough dislike of conventional texts, and a strong desire to develop and use teacher-produced texts. How could this be done? With technology. Modern desk-top publishing, as well as other computer applications, makes it possible to create your own texts. Or better yet, move beyond textbooks altogether by letting the student do it. In Orem, Utah, for instance, a Next Century School is producing algebra workbooks of its own design for 42 cents apiece. By using technology creatively, teachers in Next Century Schools across the country will be able to tease productivity increases out of an old-fashioned system and abandon boring and dated texts.

Yet if the opportunity to improve math is real, consider the social sciences in light of recent developments. Is there a school in America with a textbook, globe, or atlas that accurately reflects the changes of the last few years? If so, that school is like Piscataquis High, which uses its computers and interactive video to permit students to tap into networks and current data sets that are updated rapidly. An electronic encyclopedia is not only more interesting because it comes with still and moving pictures, color graphics, and stereo sound, but it can be updated rapidly and regularly. And it can be used interactively; students can compile their own books by downloading, integrating, and editing various current information sources. And this is just the beginning. With five to eight computers in every classroom, Piscataquis is getting more productivity out of marginal students as well; a kid who is out of sorts, far behind the class, or who otherwise acts up can be given a computer-based assignment right in the classroom. Largely self-guiding, computer-based assignments require only a modest amount of the teacher's time—or another student's—and allow the rest of the class to unfold on schedule.

Indeed, many of the problems associated with modern education are attributable to the model of mass education the textbook made possible. Large groupings of children of the same age make administrative and managerial sense, even if they make little pedagogical sense. So too periods of study, bells announcing the beginning and end of class, marks or grades, standardized tests and measures, teacher certification—all of these are examples of attempts to standardize the activity known as schooling. One of the charges given to school districts and their superintendents at the end of the nineteenth century was to "teacher-proof" the schools, and to run them just like factories with assembly lines.

Or so the early industrial engineers thought. It is now clear that the most effective factories and assembly operations are those that involve the worker in decision-making, that reward workers for contributions to increased output and improved working conditions. The modern worker in the modern plant, instead of performing mind-numbing, repetitive work, is now part of a work team, one that designs the work processes, sets goals, counsels members of the team, and on balance works better, faster, smarter, and with higher morale. Such work teams have lower absenteeism, make more money, and stay with the job longer. They are the new workforce, what *Fortune* magazine calls "workers without bosses."

Indeed, that is the hallmark of Next Century Schools; they are all institutions "without bosses." This is true not only of teachers and principals, but of superintendents as well. John Murphy, Superintendent of Charlotte-Mecklenburg schools, hopes to decentralize to 113 magnet schools by the mid-nineties, giving away power to improve education.

If it can be done in the blue-collar world of the factory, it can certainly be done in schools. However, it will be necessary to infuse schools with standards for performance. As Al Shanker notes, no country in the world has high levels of achievement unless it has high national standards; and no worker in the world, except a few dedicated people, works his best without rewards and incentives. Schools that do not make demands on students do not get results. Making demands on students is not cruel; failing to do so is. It sends them the message that they can get by with little or no effort.

It is one thing to talk about productivity increases, quite another to bring them off. And while schools and business are not the same, there are common denominators, four of which are imperative for increasing productivity:

- Know what your job is;

- Know what your outcomes should be;

- Know how you will measure output; and,

- Know what technologies and organizational formats are available to increase output.

Think of farmers, manufacturers, and service-sector workers. Each will respond to these productivity imperatives differently. Indeed, similar occupations will respond differently, depending on a variety of factors. The small farmer will not respond the way the large farmer will; the dry-land farmer will not respond the way a well-watered farmer will; but every successful farmer will deal with these imperatives.

What kinds of productivity gains might schools achieve if they took these lessons to heart? There are at least three broad areas in which major productivity gains can occur.

1. STUDENTS AS WORKERS.

When the student is defined as the worker, learning occurs not when teachers lecture or demonstrate, but when students are engaged in the learning process. It takes two to tango: a teacher and a student. Or a textbook and a student. Or a computer and a student. Or a field experience and a student. The only constant is the student. The involved and interested student. The fact is, learning is hard work, plain and simple. Satisfying, rewarding, to be sure, but hard work nonetheless. It need not be disagreeable work, but it will always require diligence, application, effort, and attentiveness. The sooner schools and students recapture this simple truism, the better. Students will be the better for it because as they develop the habit of hard work, they will be laying the foundations for adult success.

In addition to the student as worker on his or her own behalf, the student should work in the school on the school's behalf. America's fast-food industries and shopping malls are practically run by kids; there is no reason why they can't do the same, and more, in school. Kids can perform the obvious tasks—as library workers, crossing guards, clerks and data-entry technicians, buildings and grounds crews, clean-up and light maintenance, cafeteria workers, and the like. For those kids who need income, the minimum wage might be paid, but most kids should do this as a condition of graduation. Japanese schools have no janitors; students do the work. American kids are among the most pampered in the world. There's simply no reason for them not to make a contribution to their own well-being, particularly in an era characterized by perpetual budget shortfalls. And the kids will take school more seriously if they invest in it.

Even more important is the student as mentor and tutor. The opportunity to help another person learn is one of life's great pleasures, and students should know the feeling from early on. High school kids can tutor each other, or they can work with younger kids. Indeed, younger kids can often tutor older kids, or even tutor adults, as any parent who has struggled with a recalcitrant VCR knows. Frequently the kids are the real technology experts, from complicated computer programming, to running and understanding routine programs.

Many Next Century Schools have converted students into teachers. At Bell Multicultural High School in Washington, D.C., for example, students from foreign countries become instructors in their native languages. At Juanita Elementary in Seattle, Washington, nearby high school students have been enlisted as mentors for grade school children. At New Stanley Elementary and Douglas Byrd Junior High, the most adept students in each classroom tutor those who need extra help.

2. TEACHERS AS MANAGERS OF INSTRUCTION.

Making the teacher manager of instruction is more than a change of titles; it is a profound change in the way teachers work and in the way they should be paid and regarded. A manager orchestrates work effort, bringing together technology (physical capital) and people (human capital) to produce a product or service. In this case, the outcome is learning. The manager creates the environment in which learning can occur. The manager establishes incentives and disincentives, offers rewards and penalties to motivate workers. In many firms, in fact, the manager is not only the key actor, but is accountable for results.

It is up to the manager to see that the environment is conducive to work and that work occurs. The worker who can't or won't work is retrained, reassigned, or if necessary, fired. But the manager must exhaust every other option first. The manager in the effective firm is "benchmarked": A high discharge rate is a sign that the manager is not doing his or her job.

In IBM's training centers, for example, the teacher's computer instantaneously keeps track of student test scores. What happens when too many low student scores appear? Unlike most public schools, where students would be accused of failure, the assumption at IBM is that there is something wrong with the teacher's lesson plan. The interaction between teacher as manager of instruction and motivated students—students as workers—is a new kind of school!

Most important, when the teacher becomes the manager of instruction, staffing patterns and compensation will change. No longer will there be a single job description called "teacher," but there will be levels appropriate to the teacher's maturity, competence, and effectiveness, just as

246

there are in every other profession and craft. As job responsibilities change, so will compensation. Those who work longer and harder will get paid more, as they should. Not only because it is fair for them, but because they contribute more and add more value to the school. They are worth more. That's why they should be paid more. They will increase the school's output. They literally pay for themselves by doing more.

3. USE OF TECHNOLOGY.

Some schools already use technology effectively: for simple, repetitive, and tedious tasks, such as scheduling, bus routing, record keeping, ordering, and inventory control. All the things that businesses use technology for, schools may now use it for as well—at least on the "business" side of the school ledger. But schools rarely use technology to accomplish their educational and pedagogical missions. The one exception is the use of computers for "drill or practice." Yet it is precisely in the instructional realm that computers are potentially most powerful.

Next Century Schools are showing the way in this area as well. Orem High School in Orem, Utah, is developing algebra programs using computers with touch-sensitive screens and a high degree of interactivity. The computers will be networked, providing the users access to a remote server and providing the teacher with a way to reach students electronically. At the same time, the teacher may use the interactive network to monitor student progress. It is possible, for example, to find out which algebra problems prove especially troublesome, or especially clear and easy to solve, and to track the frequency with which students deal with them.

The real power of technology, of course, it to leverage "smart work," from the journalist with the word processor to the scientist with the Cray supercomputer. For white-collar workers the communications revolution is simply stunning: fax machines, lap-tops, satellite up and down links, and cellular telephones. We are beginning to see schools take advantage of these technologies as well, from telephone hotlines for homework to the use of fax machines for information exchange.

Most exciting, however, are schools that use computers to increase the rate at which students learn and the depth of coverage they are able to achieve. Such computer use is not restricted to high schools; Rummel Creek, in Houston, Texas, for example, has put in place an elementary school version of a university. In place of conventional age and ability groupings, Rummel Creek students will take a series of courses, including electives, just as college students do. More difficult courses will have prerequisites that students must first satisfy. And the delivery system is a networked computer system; every child in the school has a computer on his or her desk, just as every teacher and administrator does.

Rappahannock Elementary School in Sperryville, Virginia, in conjunction with its corporate partners, Xerox and Pepco, has a computer for every fourth-grader to accelerate and deepen math-skill acquisition. Building on demonstrated success with sixth-graders, Rappahannock is deliberately using computer technology to increase productivity, one part of its commitment to total quality management.

A Call for Action

Of all the themes in this book, productivity is probably the most foreign to educators. Indeed, most people think of schools as warm, well-lighted places where productivity, if it is thought about at all, is a subject of study, not a commitment to action. However, American schools now face a productivity crisis. They must learn to do more with what they have, for two reasons. It is entirely possible that schools will not be able to exert a successful claim on any more of society's resources. The competition may simply be too fierce, particularly as the population ages, as incomes continue to diverge, and as the nation suburbanizes. Schools may well be stuck with the resources now at their disposal. However, it is equally clear that schools will never be able to claim the resources they would like unless they can demonstrate to the satisfaction of parents and taxpayers that they are productive organizations. When the public is satisfied that it is getting value for its tax dollars, the public is generous.

If it is any consolation to educators, the same issue arises in all our social services, from garbage collection to medicine. Indeed, it is impossible to imagine a reasoned discussion about any social service without attending to the question of cost containment. It is simply part of the equation, and schools cannot escape.

Is there some good in the situation in which public schools now find themselves, as labor-intensive, low-tech institutions? There is. Schools are so low-tech and labor-intensive that they have no place to go but up. The good news is that there is enormous slack in the system. There is ample room for significant productivity gains. Making students workers and teachers managers of instruction, and using technology to get more for less, will transform schools,

249

from low-performance to high-performance organizations. This is precisely what the nation needs for the twenty-first century.

Our schools supported the greatest industrial economy the world has ever known. They can support the greatest postindustrial economy in the world as well. For our trump card, the real American genius, is our inventiveness, our resourcefulness, our irreverence, and our willingness to jettison tradition for new ways of doing things. Schools, unfortunately, tend to judge themselves on how hard they try, not how well they do. Schools must learn to focus on goals; they must no longer fall into the trap of measuring inputs rather than outputs, or they will fall into the worst trap of all: meaning well and doing poorly.

CHAPTER 10

Assignment America: Take Back Our Schools

Our people can't be properly trained unless they are first adequately educated. . . . We are running out of time and no less than the future of the nation is at stake.

—James Burke, Chairman
Johnson & Johnson

Imagine, for a moment, a great revival of American public schools early in the next century:

> Across the country, schoolchildren are thriving. News stories trumpet the performance gains of American youth compared to their older siblings and parents. Drop-out rates are down. International test score comparisons show sharp improvements for U.S. children. From Japan and Europe, educators and legislators arrive to tour the best of these remarkably successful institutions, and to learn the secrets of their stunning renewal in the 1990s.
>
> These visitors from abroad are particularly intrigued by the way in which U.S. schools have regained their capacity to socialize and educate millions of children from diverse backgrounds, especially those whose families speak little English, or whose parents are poor and uneducated.
>
> Some visitors are impressed with American measurement systems, and goal-setting processes. Others marvel at the advanced instructional technology; still others study the dramatic changes that have been

made in how U.S. schools are organized, staffed, and led.

But in trying to understand the new American educational reforms, foreign visitors are confused. Like previous stories of American success, there does not seem to be one story, but many. Indeed, the revival of America's schools is astoundingly diverse. There is no national curriculum, no single system of computerization, no uniform criteria for school hours, or teacher credentials, or textbooks. Rather, there are thousands of schools, with thousands of strategies. America seems to have transformed its schools one at a time.

The changes have come not because a federal law was passed, or a national blueprint adopted, but because millions of individuals in tens of thousands of communities took action. Like the interactive computers and software that swept into the schools in the 1990s (as they had earlier swept into America's offices), the revolution in American schools is a social phenomenon, not a concerted plan. One by one, America's schools have been reborn.

This is not a far-fetched vision.

Only a few decades ago, American public schools were considered marvels of excellence, and keys to America's world leadership. In the 1960s, America's schools were envied, and copied by many of the world's nations. Today, Americans want their schools to be envied again; American parents want superb public schools. There is no reason this cannot be accomplished. Americans are rich enough to afford top schools, smart enough to create them, and dedicated enough to sustain them. Our schools can be great again.

But if this dream is to come true, enormous energy and resolve must be focused on these tarnished institutions. And many individuals and organizations must change their habits and assumptions. What was good enough in the 1950s and 1960s is not good enough today. The traditional factory organization of schools must be abandoned. The vast web of bureaucracy and regulation that ensnares teachers and principals must be swept away. New ways must be found to hire talented teachers and principals; new standards must be set for testing and motivating students. New investments must be made in the parents and communities of poor children.

What if we fail to take these steps? What will the future look like if nothing, or little, is done? That future is already partly visible in many cities and towns in America: middle-class parents giving up on public schools and fleeing to economically segregated suburbs or private schools; big-city school systems becoming holding pens for untutored children, and sinecures for incompetent teachers and administrators; ever greater divisions between society's rich and educated, and poor and uneducated; a vicious downward spiral of lagging school performance, postponed school spending, and defeated bond issues; a fundamental loss of faith in public schools and their ability to uplift disadvantaged people; growing doubt that America can hold its place in the world.

The task of transforming this dark vision into a bright future for public schools will be difficult, but it is not insurmountable. Next Century Schools, psychologist Jim Comer's Effective Schools, Ted Sizer's Essential Schools, Stanford Professor Henry Levin's Accelerated Schools, and the nine winners of New American Schools Development Corporation awards, are among the most well-known examples of excellence in public schooling. They are blazing a trail for others to follow, and countless cities and towns are defining lofty education goals as they look to the future.

If these pathbreakers are to be emulated, many people must act. School by school, parents, teachers, and citizens-at-large must change our schools.

What must be done if foreign visitors in the next century are to marvel at America's school revival? How will a school-by-school revolution take place? If a rebirth of American public schools happens in the 1990s, visitors to American schools in the next century will surely find schools that look much like Next Century Schools. Certain features of school improvement will show up over and over again in the stories told by school principals and teachers, by parents and administrators. In virtually every successful school, foreign visitors will find five things:

- A dynamic, communicative principal, with great freedom to lead his or her school toward a vision of educational excellence;

- A rigorous set of school goals, and a system in place for measuring progress toward them;

- A cadre of competent teachers, whose enthusiasm is multiplied by their use of many advanced education tools and technologies;

- Students who are workers—engaged, enthusiastic, and hard-working; and

- An engaged group of parents, supported by a vigorous program that directly involves them in the school.

What actions must be taken to make these things happen, and who must take them?

Nothing matters more for the future of American public schools than finding great principals to lead them. If it were possible to wave a magic wand and place America's best 83,000 leaders in charge of its 83,000 public schools, the school crisis would soon be behind us. Bold leaders that can help shape a vision and motivate students, teachers, and parents to achieve it are critically needed in every American school.

Although no one can wave such a wand, many can make a difference. The greatest responsibility belongs to school-district administrators, and in some cases to local school boards—those with direct authority to hire principals. Despite the personal pain, and the political risks, those responsible for school systems must accept the greatest challenge of their jobs: recruiting individuals with leadership capability, and moving aside those who lack it.

In large or small school systems, the decision to change a school principal often ignites emotional, personal, and political battles. School principals in many districts have enjoyed something equivalent to university tenure; individuals are seldom removed except for serious misconduct, and many stay in their jobs for years or decades. Most school district administrators, along with parents, teachers, and the principals themselves expect school principals to stay in their jobs until retirement. Suggestions that this traditional stability be changed are often greeted with anger and hostility.

But while long tenure is comfortable for principals and school-district administrators, it is not good for schools or children. Vital institutions change their leadership regularly. Institutions like the military or large businesses typically expect managers or leaders to occupy the same job for only a

257

few years before they receive new assignments. This institutionalized turnover in leadership positions is intended to inject new thinking, new relationships, and new techniques into the organization. School systems must adopt the same philosophy.

Yet only a few district administrators are brave enough to fire principals, and they often put themselves in jeopardy by doing so. During the five years that John Murphy was superintendent of schools in Prince George's County, Maryland, he replaced more than half the principals in the county school system. When he moved to Charlotte, North Carolina, he replaced 41 of 113 principals by the end of his first year on the job. The process of changing school leadership is wrenching for everyone involved. But the benefits of shaking up the status quo and bringing strong new leaders into the schools that need them are worth the pain.

Before school-district leaders have the freedom and the guts to hire great principals, however, they must be given the mandate, and the support they need to act. Before school districts can hire great principals, they must hire strong district leaders, and back them up. Sadly, the incredibly demanding job of being superintendent of schools is often filled by a cautious bureaucrat, who can get fired for stepping out of line. Though administrators of large school districts may manage thousands of people, and hundreds of millions of dollars, they are paid moderate salaries (relative to their responsibilities) and are subject to intense fiscal, political, and bureaucratic pressures.

The first reform, then, that would enable districts to hire talented principals, is to empower able school-district leaders. School boards, like corporate boards, have as their first, most urgent priority the creation of a package of compensation, challenges, accountability, and responsibility that will at-

258

tract talented chief executives. Then they must give those executives power—charge them with responsibility to build their management cadre, one school building at a time.

The metaphor of corporate governance in which the board delegates executive power to a CEO has other parallels for school districts seeking to restructure themselves and their schools. Although corporate boards have been criticized for exerting too little control over corporate executives, the opposite is true of most school boards: They impose far too much detailed oversight. Like well-run corporations, school districts must find ways to delegate more power from headquarters to the field. Specifically, school boards should explicitly delegate personnel and budget decisions to the CEO—the superintendent—who in turn should delegate authority to schools. For example, school boards should not set detailed policies governing the hiring of teachers or establishing formulas assigning "slots" for support personnel or cafeteria or custodial workers. These decisions are made most sensibly at the building level, as they now are in many Next Century Schools. School boards should establish budget priorities as general allocations, and they should establish broad guidelines for detailed implementation by the superintendent and school principals.

Principals should be free to hire the best people for the job, and to allocate expenditures within their budgets. By giving budget and hiring authority to schools themselves, central offices can enable principals and teachers to invest resources—as needed—to educate children. Indeed, school principals should not be required to use district staff offices for services such as procurement, hiring, operations, or other needs if these can be obtained elsewhere more cheaply or effectively. There are firms that can provide schools with bus service, record-keeping, cafeteria management, recruitment, training, or virtually any other service they may need, on a competitive basis.

Most organizations make conscious decisions about those tasks they will undertake themselves, and those they will ask others to do for them. School systems should do the same, focusing their efforts on teaching children, and contracting for the other services they need. Of course, many schools may elect to continue to use district offices for these services. But the option to ignore the front office will be a powerful tonic for performance, and a powerful stimulus for change and efficiency.

This vision of radical decentralization of power and control to school-building leaders may seem hopelessly naive to people who are familiar with the ponderous, politically entrenched bureaucracies of school systems. But decentralization *can* be achieved, even in the face of overwhelming bureaucratic opposition. When General Motors faced huge losses in the mid 1980s, it managed just such a radical decentralization with the creation of its Saturn subsidiary. Like today's schools, General Motors is a centralized organization with elaborate systems for controlling costs, preventing errors, and covering up mistakes. When the Saturn project was unveiled, knowledgeable insiders scoffed at the idea of completely reinventing the organization, delegating virtually all decisions to the new Saturn group. But faced with an eroding market share and fierce international competition, the firm managed to break with its past. Those who control school districts must be prepared to contemplate equally radical steps.

The Saturn story also contains lessons for how the various participants can help to bring about change in the structure of school systems. Before the Saturn plant could come into being, many parties shared in the planning of the new enterprise, and in the process were required to sacrifice traditional prerogatives. Thousands of GM employees gave up their homes and jobs to move to the new facilities in Tennessee. Unions renegotiated agreements. Dealers and parts suppliers accepted new contract terms. Every accepted idea and standard operating procedure for designing, making, and selling cars was reexamined.

A similar approach is possible in public schools. In the early 1990s, as part of the process of developing blueprints for becoming *America 2000* communities, (or through other district-wide planning processes), school districts have had the opportunity to reexamine the traditional organization and structure of their schools. One goal of this review should be to push real authority and responsibility as far down into schools and classrooms as possible.

Two years ago, the Charlotte-Mecklenburg School District began a planning process that could become a model for the nation. Superintendent John Murphy had been given a mandate to pursue excellence in the district's schools, and he kicked off a process intended to mobilize the community on behalf of massive change. The process involved a series of meetings with various constituencies, including teachers, students, the business community, and parent and community groups. It established a concrete vision of the school system toward which the district is striving, and promoted the development of specific standards for teachers, principals, parents, and students. Ultimately, the district intends to create a system of 113 magnet schools, each virtually autonomous, subject only to performance standards. One way of describing what is happening in Charlotte is that the district headquarters is working to put itself out of business.

At the same time that authorities in school districts, in legislatures, and in Washington must relinquish power to schools, principals and teachers must prepare themselves to wield it. Today, most of those who are on the front lines in public schools lack the skills and the will to take control of their own futures. Among the thousands of proposals submitted to the RJR Nabisco Foundation asking for money, few contained sensible budgets, a clear idea of priorities, or well-thought-out operating plans. Even schools that won found themselves scrambling to develop their capacities to manage money and people, to set standards for themselves, and to monitor their results. Like lions born in captivity, they had never learned to fend for themselves.

Preparing schools to manage their own affairs could be expedited by revamped teacher colleges working in cooperation with schools of business management. Instead of the traditional education courses, schools preparing educators should develop courses that cover a broader range of subjects: budgeting, communications, management of small groups, leadership, quality assessment. As the well-run public school adopts the techniques and organization of the well-run company, the skills needed by its employees will come more and more to resemble the skills used elsewhere in the workplace.

Nobel laureate in economics Milton Freidman was asked to address a gathering of the party elite of China in 1989 as the winds of change were beginning to sweep over the communist world. The theme of his talk was how market systems could be employed within the context of the centralized planning system to promote greater production and efficiency. Friedman opened his remarks with a simple suggestion: "Gentlemen, disband." There was no way, Friedman argued, to use market systems within the old framework; the centralized system itself was the problem. His prophetic words could be applied as well to America's large, centrally planned public school systems. The structure of the system itself must be changed.

If delegating authority is one side of the coin, the flip side is demanding accountability. Schools that have been given money and power to act on behalf of children must be held responsible for the children's performance.

Responsibility for developing standards and measures—accountability—rests with local and national leaders. At the local level, every school district must engage in systematic goal-setting to clarify parent, teacher, student, and principal expectations. Goals obviously will vary from community to community, because parents want their children to learn different things, and because different children have different backgrounds. In barrio schools of East Los Angeles, Hispanic parents may expect more emphasis on Spanish literacy for fourth-graders than will native English speakers from wealthy Santa Maria; but all youngsters must master English, even if it takes longer for some students than others.

Locally and nationally, there must be room for multiple stakeholders, not just parents. Local businesses and civic leaders have the right and responsibility to specify clearly what they expect. Teachers, who are the most knowledgeable and most committed participants, have a special role in the setting of realistic goals, to which they will be held accountable.

Students, especially those at the high school level, also have a central role in setting standards and developing ways to measure progress. In Charlotte-Mecklenburg and in several other Next Century Schools, students have often been the most forthright and well-informed critics of the quality of the teaching in their schools, as well as being ready with suggestions for how to improve it.

In order to jump-start the local school-planning processes, federal funding should be more flexible. Instead of detailed regulations limiting Chapter One expenditures for the disadvantaged, new regulations should simply require that each school district undertake a planning effort to decide how to use the money most effectively.

A local planning process that describes local differences in standards and expectations must be benchmarked against international standards that are established by national authorities. A single set of national education goals must be developed, that can peg individual and local performance at certain age or grade levels, and allow it to be compared to national norms. Importantly, these standards should be both criterion-referenced, allowing specific descriptions of what students know and how they perform on certain tasks, and norm-referenced, permitting comparisons with other schools and students.

National education groups should be charged with the responsibility for developing these tests and standards, including benchmarking students from different cultures and backgrounds. There is no substitute for a yardstick that will enable every school, every classroom, and every child to be measured against every other. The first steps have already been taken in mathematics by the National Council of Teachers of Mathematics; other national umbrella groups are following, and they should be strongly encouraged to continue their work.

Goals and standards are only as good as the tests that are used to evaluate progress. The great weakness of school reform today is that current standardized tests fail to measure many important skills, and may encourage students and teachers to focus too much on rote knowledge. Schools held accountable for test results often complain they spend too much time in useless "teaching to the test," filling their students with textbook details and test-taking skills, and not enough in developing creativity and critical thinking skills. As one educator put it, "We need a national test that's worth teaching to."

It is imperative that the nation have a set of tests that are "worth teaching to." Combining the curriculum standards of national teacher groups and the technology skills of large computer makers and software firms with the advice of psychometrians and other experts under a national, or international, umbrella group is the way to proceed. Such a group, funded from the federal education research budget, should include representatives from every affected constituency: teachers, parents, students, unions, business, governors, and legislators. Their mandate should be straightforward: Develop and validate a set of tests that will measure where our students stand and help to guide their educational development and the management of their schools. Then publish test results that will show how each district and school in the country compares to others in similar circumstances, and to all schools.

Human capital is the engine of modern economic growth. In schools, teachers are the key to performance and school success. What must be done to ensure that schools are staffed with teachers who have the skills, the motivation, and the tools to do their jobs well? Who must take action?

Again, heavy responsibility falls on those who set hiring and training policies: school boards and administrative officials. The chief message from Next Century Schools to these officials is simple: Get out of the way. If schools are competently led, and teachers and principals are given primary responsibility for defining their own goals and the means for accomplishing them, they will succeed. Most of the "assistance" provided to teachers by school administrators is unnecessary or counterproductive. Specifically, school administrators and state officials would be better served by eliminating most of the rules governing hiring in public schools, and by delegating to schools themselves responsibility for deciding whom to hire, what jobs they should do, and how they should do them.

In particular, the elaborate system of state standards established to license teachers should be repealed. One alternative would be to adopt the national competency-based standards that are being developed by the National Board for Professional Teaching Standards. The NBPTS, jointly funded by the Congress, the Carnegie Endowment for Teaching, and others (including the RJR Nabisco Foundation), is dedicated to defining a set of standards for professional teachers that would allow them to be certified just as doctors in certain specialties are certified by independent boards. Importantly, these standards are not being based on credentials conferred or coursework taken, but on demonstrated ability and experience teaching children. Professional teachers would be certified based on portfolios of work, in-class evaluations, and other demonstrations of performance. Ideally, these open-ended national standards will eventually replace state licensing requirements that currently restrict entrance into teaching.

In some jurisdictions, deregulating teacher hiring will be impossible without reopening collective bargaining agreements. Reopen them. Teacher unions should have a voice in their profession. Of all those involved with public schools, teachers have the most to gain from radical restructuring of schools. Fundamental reforms can lead to vibrant, successful schools, which are the only guarantee of public support, job security, and decent pay for teachers. School-based management, including open hiring policies, will return management of schools to the people who work in them.

But if teacher unions are to play a constructive role in re-defining the teaching profession, they must accept a redefinition of their own goals. Teacher unions do not represent craftsmen or tradesmen, and the goal of collective bargaining is not simply higher wages across the board. Teacher unions represent professionals. Like other professionals, they should be in favor of pay scales that reflect differences in competence and differences in market conditions. Teachers who push students to learn should receive more than teachers who bore students into quitting school. Like the professionals they represent, teacher unions should be fighting for better tools to work with in the classroom, including computers, phones, and all the instruments of the information age. If teachers are to be paid in part based on performance, then they should demand that they be equipped with the tools they need to be productive. Just as a teacher without books is disadvantaged, a teacher without computers, advanced software, and other tools is handicapped. Teacher unions should have a large say in how classrooms are computerized and how compensation rates are established.

The institutions that educate America's teachers also must radically reshape their roles, if they are to support the goal of a revitalized teaching profession. As the skills needed in teaching come more to resemble those found elsewhere in the workplace, so schools that educate teachers must shift toward training that has wide applicability. Teachers need to be familiar with instructional technology; they need training in presentation skills; they must know more about the management of small groups, and be able to assume a variety of leadership roles. Some of these skills may be learned in courses borrowed from schools of business. Others may be developed in practicums or supervised training programs.

In undertaking reform, schools of education would be well advised to listen to their customers: schools and teachers. Today they often fail to serve those customers, instead offering elaborate courses whose only justification is that they are required for certification. If there were no certification or continuing education requirements, but simply budgets that local schools could invest in teacher training, schools of education would be forced to respond much differently. Courses would be shorter and livelier (measured in days and hours, not weeks and months), addressing issues of direct concern to classroom practitioners. Technology would undoubtedly be taught more and used more. Instruction would be moved into the schools themselves, or delivered on-demand, electronically, to teachers in their schools or homes.

Reforms in teacher recruitment and training cannot take place unless schools are given greater budgetary freedom. Without flexibility to transfer resources from, for example, payroll accounts to software purchases, or to change pupil-teacher child ratios to accommodate more planning time, or to teach sixth-grade math with a different mix of people and machines compared to eighth-grade history, schools will never be able to manage their people more productively.

Various successful NCS experiments run the gamut from almost pure investments in computer hardware and software development, to pure payroll increases reflected in higher pupil-teacher ratios, to purchasing extra time for teachers to plan together and train themselves. Unless all schools have the same flexibility to maximize their own mix of people, tools, and training, they will not achieve the gains that are possible.

Schools control a small fraction of each student's time and attention. What a child learns at home, and in his or her community, is often more influential than what is taught in school. When schools are filled with the children of middle-class, educated parents, these outside influences are beneficial. When children come from the homes of the poor and poorly educated, the schools struggle uphill against terrible odds.

As Next Century Schools and many other schools have proven, there are ways to overcome these odds—to take school into the community, to educate parents about their responsibilities to their children, to provide additional services to children who need them, and to bring parents into the schools to learn and to teach. These programs to reach out into children's homes and communities—to use school as a counterweight to the negative effects of the home and community—have often been remarkably effective. Such programs have only two common denominators: They require a much greater commitment from the school to children, and they cost money.

If teachers are to visit homes, if mentors are to be recruited for children without parents, if health and social services are to be provided in the school, it will require staff time, facilities, and money. If children from uneducated families are to start school even with middle-class kids, it will require new, expensive programs. If children who fall behind or lose hope in school are to be provided with special tutors or special programs to recapture success for them, it will require intensive effort and new resources.

Many argue that schools should stick to the job of education, and allow other programs and institutions to undertake these social responsibilities. Schools cannot be all things to all people. But if America wishes to rebuild its decayed cities, overcome the destructive effects of underclass behavior and beliefs, make productive citizens of millions of poorly educated immigrants, and finally erase the destructive legacy of centuries of racism, the only institution that can perform the task is the schools. Public schools are the only public institution capable of making the lives of children different from, and better than, the lives of their parents. A failure to expand the role of schools to include responsibility for the welfare of children is a decision to avoid the problem.

To put the issue of America's underclass behind us, we must strengthen the capacity—and funding—of the public schools in our poorest ghettos. To do so will take action from many levels.

Most importantly, state and federal legislators must channel more resources to these schools, and enable schools to invest in a broad array of social services. In some cases, money can be reprogrammed from other uses, or targeted more tightly on the schools that need it most. For example, federal funds should flow to schools in need; "rich" districts can make it on their own. So long as Chapter One is not fully funded, it will be necessary to pressure the Congress to find funds for it.

But new money for poor school districts must be a two-way bargain. A public alarmed by deficits, tired of tax increases, and skeptical of government's ability to work efficiently will be reluctant to support new funding for public schools. This will be especially so in the case of tax dollars that must flow from rich to poor districts, or from the federal to the local level. Unless schools are willing to be held accountable for their performance, and to manage themselves efficiently, they will be starved for funds. No one wants to simply pour more money into districts with lax school administrators and layers of bureaucracy. To the maximum extent feasible, new money for services in poor school districts should go directly to schools with as little overhead and as few restrictions as possible. Schools should be held accountable for how they spend the money and rewarded for the success they achieve in improving the lives of children.

Others can help to fund and support these efforts by

schools to do more for children. Business, for example, has a responsibility to shift resources—both money and volunteer help—to the schools that need it most. While business cannot be expected to support regular operating and capital expenditures (which should be paid for out of public budgets), they can help pay for innovation, investments in new programs, and experiments that can be replicated with public funds.

Assignments for Reinventing Our Schools

To conclude this sketch of what needs to be done and who should do it, it is worth recapitulating the assignments that must be undertaken if America is to reinvent and revitalize its schools:

- *School-district leaders:* Seek out great leaders for public schools, and then delegate responsibility for managing schools, including budget and hiring powers, to them.

- *State legislators and governors:* Clear away the thicket of restrictions that bind school systems, set performance standards, and provide new funding for schools from poor districts.

- *Federal legislators and leaders:* Underwrite the development of curriculum standards, provide incentives for local planning, and develop tests for measuring school performance. Federal resources should be reallocated to poor schools that will undertake a broader array of services to children.

- *Teachers:* Prepare yourselves to take charge of your own schools by investing in your own capacities to

271

teach, change, and lead, and by systematically planning the changes you wish to see in your schools.

- *Schools of education* in cooperation with *schools of business:* Reform the way you teach teachers, focusing more on skills such as communication, management, and use of technology.

- *Business:* Advise schools what you expect students to learn, help them manage themselves effectively, and contribute people and money to assist them in making changes.

- *Teacher unions:* Accept the challenge of professionalizing teaching, including negotiating much greater flexibility in hiring rules, designing merit pay systems, and welcoming the introduction of technology.

- *Parents and taxpayers:* Insist that you be included in local planning efforts, spend time inside your schools, support investments in schools for other people's children, and insist on high standards and measured results.

- *Principals:* Use participatory processes to establish a vision for your school; seek the best teachers you can find, and give them the tools and the freedom they need to do their jobs; and above all, listen to, and communicate with, teachers, parents, and students.

- *Students:* grasp the fact that you are workers; school is life, not a dress rehearsal.

The secret of reinventing American schools will be found in a medley of practices most Americans think of as unique to the private, not the public sector. They include a variety of processes, practices, rewards, incentives, and opportunities once thought of as the exclusive province of markets. But if the twentieth century teaches anything, it is that freedom—political and economic—is the hallmark of personal dignity, national security, and economic growth. Schools are no exception to this general rule. Our purpose in telling this story—Reinventing Education: Entrepreneurship in America's Public Schools—has been to demonstrate that complex social organizations—for-profit and not-for-profit, private and public—have much in common. Each can—and must—learn from the other.

For example, "public-sector" market mechanisms can serve the same function in schools as they serve in the private sector: sending signals about good and bad practice; rewarding success; penalizing failure; guaranteeing the sovereignty of the customer; and providing a continuing responsibility to benchmark. Benchmarking, a practice developed by modern business, is no less and no more than comparing yourself to the best of the best. It requires merciless and regular self-examination; it requires providers to meet the needs and demands of customers; it sets the stage for fruitful, not invidious, comparison. It is the key to quality.

American schools were once the best in the world. They will be again, because Americans will countenance no less.

From the colonists who set out from England in the seventeenth century, to the technological wizards of Silicon Valley, the great strength of Americans has always been our willingness to change. Now we must change again. Our public schools that worked so well only a few years ago have become trapped by outmoded traditions and blundering bureaucracies. They are not serving us well now, and they cannot survive intact into the next century. One by one, we must reinvent our schools.

ABOUT THE AUTHORS

Louis V. Gerstner, Jr., is the Chairman and Chief Executive Officer of the IBM Corporation. Prior to that he was Chairman and CEO of RJR Nabisco, and Chairman of the RJR Nabisco Foundation and the Next Century Schools Advisory Board. As president of the American Express Company and Chairman and Chief Executive Officer of its Travel Related Services subsidiary, Mr. Gerstner headed the National Academy Foundation. He has also served as chairman of the Joint Council on Economic Education and as a member of the Harvard Business School Visiting Committee, the board of trustees of the International Management Institute Foundation (Geneva), and the Business-Higher Education Forum.

Mr. Gerstner received his bachelor's degree from Dartmouth College in 1964 and an M.B.A. from Harvard Business School. He lives with his wife, Robin Gerstner, in Connecticut; they are the parents of a son and daughter.

Roger D. Semerad, former Senior Vice President of RJR Nabisco, served as a counselor and strategist on a broad scope of human capital issues that affected the company, and was president of the RJR Nabisco Foundation. He served on the National Council on Education Standards and Testing and the Secretary's Commission on Achieving Necessary Skills. He is a member of the Hudson Institute Board of Trustees and The Bryce Harlow Foundation Board, and is the Treasurer of the New American Schools Development Corporation. Before joining RJR Nabisco, Mr. Semerad was Senior Vice President for Policy Development at the American Express Company.

His interest in education issues and the necessity to prepare Americans for the workforce dates back to 1966, when he was named a Fellow with the U.S. Office of Education. Since then, he has served as an aide to Presidents Nixon and Ford with Domestic Council responsibility for education, labor, and veterans affairs. He also served on the National Advisory Council on Vocational Education, and was Assistant Secretary of Labor for Employment and Training, where he was responsible for the Job Training Partnership Act, the United States Employment Service, the Job Corps, and the Bureau of Apprenticeship and Training.

Mr. Semerad is a graduate of Union College and completed active military service in 1962. He and his wife, Kate, are parents of a married daughter, Samantha.

Denis Philip Doyle, an education consultant, speaker, and author, is a Senior Fellow at the Hudson Institute. He was formerly the Director of Education Policy Studies and Human Capital Studies at the American Enterprise Institute. Prior to his tenure at AEI he was a Federal Executive Fellow at the Brookings Institution. He has held several government posts, including Assistant Director of the National Institute of Education and Assistant Director, United States Office of Economic Opportunity, and is a member of the National Education Commission on Time and Learning.

Mr. Doyle is widely published, with numerous articles to

his credit. His op-ed pieces appear regularly in *The Wall Street Journal, The Washington Post, The Los Angeles Times, The Baltimore Sun,* and *Education Week.* He also appears in the *Phi Delta Kappan, American Educator, Teachers College Record, The New York Times, The Atlantic, The Public Interest,* and the *Wilson Quarterly.* He has co-authored five books on education, including *Winning the Brain Race: A Bold Plan to Make Our Schools Competitive,* with David T. Kearns.

Mr. Doyle earned his bachelor's and master's degrees in political theory from the University of California at Berkeley in 1962 and 1964. He lives in Chevy Chase, Maryland, and is married to Gloria Revilla Doyle; they are the parents of a daughter, Alicia, and a son, Christopher.

William B. Johnston is currently Executive Vice President of Burson-Marsteller, and a member of the RJR Nabisco Foundation's Next Century Schools Advisory Board. As a Senior Fellow at the Hudson Institute, he co-authored the report *Workforce 2000,* a project that focused on trends that affect workers and their jobs in the late twentieth century. He has published extensively on labor market economics, telecommunications, and transportation issues. His articles have appeared in numerous newspapers and magazines including *The Wall Street Journal, The New York Times, The Washington Post, Fortune,* and the *Monthly Labor Review.* He was formerly the Director of Public Policy Research for the Conference Board, Assistant Secretary for Policy and International Affairs of the U.S. Department of Transportation, the Associate Director of the White House Policy Staff, and a research fellow at the George Washington Center for Social Policy Studies.

He received a bachelor's degree from Yale University. He and his wife, Jingle, a geologist, are the parents of two daughters who attend public schools in Virginia.

ACKNOWLEDGMENTS

We owe our colleagues on the Next Century Schools Advisory Board a special debt of gratitude, both for their service to the board—the cause of school reform—and for making this book possible. Because Next Century Schools was designed as a radical school reform and renewal program, we were determined to put together an advisory board that would be both visionary and practical, composed of men and women who understood the need to change and the politics of change.

The original Next Century Schools Advisory Board included former Governor of Arkansas, President Bill Clinton. It also included two men who later became the leaders of President Bush's education team: former Tennessee Governor, University of Tennessee President, and Secretary of Education, Lamar Alexander; and former Xerox CEO and Chairman, and Deputy Secretary of Education, David Kearns. Former Governor of New Jersey, Thomas Kean, who is currently President of Drew University, also serves on the board, as do Albert Shanker, President of the American Federation of Teachers, and Keith Geiger, President of the National Education Association.

Former Deputy Commissioner of the U.S. Department of

Education (the first woman to hold the position), and former D.C. Superintendent of Schools, Floretta McKenzie, is a member, as is Dick Beattie, former General Counsel to the Department of Health, Education and Welfare. In addition to a private law practice, Beattie also serves as the Chairman of the Fund for New York City Public Education.

Nationally recognized author and policy analyst— *America in Ruins* and *The High Flex Society*—Pat Choate is an Advisory Board member. He is joined by Dick Heckert, retired Chairman and CEO of E. I. du Pont de Nemours and Company, Inc., where he continues as a member of the board and also serves on the Carnegie Institution Board of Trustees.

Vernon Jordan, a partner in the Washington, D.C., law firm of Akin, Gump, Strauss, Hauer & Feld, former president of the National Urban League, and a trustee of The Brookings Institution, The American Express Corporation, RJR Nabisco and Xerox Corporation, brings his wisdom and vast experience to the Advisory Board.

Ann Mclaughlin, former Secretary of Labor—where she established the Commission on Workforce Quality and Labor Market Efficiency—served on the Next Century Schools Advisory Board until her appointment, July 1, 1992, as President and CEO of the New American Schools Development Corporation. Patricia Graham, former dean of the Harvard Graduate School of Education, and current President of the Spencer Foundation, is on the Advisory Board, as is Ted Sizer, former dean of the Harvard Graduate School of Education, founder of the Coalition of Essential Schools program, and author of *Horace's Compromise*.

The most recent Advisory Board member is Jim Hunt, Governor of North Carolina and a national leader in education reform since his first term in 1977. His vision led to the creation of the North Carolina School of Science and Mathematics in 1979, one of the nation's premier public schools. He helped establish and serves as Chairman of the National Board of Professional Teaching Standards.

A book of this kind is the product of many hands and many minds. Obviously, any mistakes or omissions are the responsibility of the authors. Equally, the richness of the text—particularly the anecdotes that bring dry reporting to life—are the product of many "reporters" and observers. RJR Nabisco Foundation staff and consultants have provided us with much of our raw material. We are specifically indebted to David Dawley, Joellen Shiffman, Donna Stelling, and Laura Allen, who were involved from the beginning in selecting the winning Next Century Schools, as well as monitoring their progress over time.

In addition, we could not have brought either the Next Century Schools program or this book to completion without the efforts of Floretta McKenzie (in her capacity as the Next Century Schools oversight contractor, as well as a Next Century Schools Advisory Board member) and her staff: Janis Cromer, Douglass Gordon, Lois Hopson, David Huie, Ann Meyer, Robert Peebles, John Rankin, Betsy Steinberger, and Zollie Stevenson. To them we extend our thanks.

We also wish to thank Amy Liker, who brought the manuscript together, both substantively and logistically. Without her long hours, unfailing patience, and good humor, this book would never have seen the light of day.

INDEX

Index

Marketing, 39–40, 48
  leadership and, 132–33
Market segmentation, 39, 41–42
Marshall Early Learning Center, 145–46
Mass-produced education, 231–32, 242
Mastery learning, 121–22, 126, 183
  measuring, by levels of accomplishment,
    188–91, 196
  standards for, 189–91
Mathematics, 64–65, 69, 152–53, 241, 247,
  264
Mavis Beacon's Typing Tutor, 37, 57
Meadows, Anita, 158
Meadows, Suzanne, 158
Measurement of progress toward goals,
  69–70, 103–14, 264–65
Merit Scholarships, 5, 6
Middle class, 199–200, 211, 268–69
Middle Tennessee State College, 207
Migration and education, 200, 210–11
Milikanized schools, 45
Military Academy, U.S., 119–20
Milliken, Bill, 220
Minority students, 7, 22, 45, 49, 100
  culture and, 186, 187, 211–13
  immigrant, 83
  integration and, 45, 49
  leadership and, 127–28
  mobile classroom and, 98
  standardized testing of, 106–107, 230
  violence and, 208
  vouchers and, 23
Mobile classrooms, 98
"Models for Change" class, 161
Mokyr, Joel, 234
Molholm Elementary School, 214–15
Monopolies, 25–26, 33
  "creative destruction" and, 58
  "naturally occurring," 39
Montessori schools, 39
Morgan County Elementary School, 101
  school readiness and, 203
Motivation, 32–33
  increasing, 194–95
  self-, 213
Motorola, 10
Moynihan, Daniel Patrick, 197, 200–201
Murphrysboro, Tennessee, 207–208
Murphy, John, 28, 45, 115, 195, 215–17, 243,
  258, 261
Murray, June, 143
Murry Bergtraum High School, 30, 219

Nadeau, Adel, 166
Nathan Hale Junior High School, 130,
  164–65, 194
National Academy Foundation, ix

National Assessment of Educational Prog-
  ress (NAEP), 7, 191
National Association of Secondary School
  Principals, 214
National Board for Professional Teaching
  Standards (NBPTS), 266
National Children's Policy, 224
National Council of Teachers of Mathemat-
  ics, 264
National Council on Education Standards
  and Testing, 105–106
National Education Association, 166, 175
National Education Commission on Time
  and Learning, 78
National Governors' Association, 22
National standardized testing, 105–14
Nation at Risk, A, 11
Native Americans, 186, 187
Naval Academy, U.S., 37–38, 119–20
New American Schools Development Cor-
  poration awards, 255–56
New relationship among schools, parents,
  and communities, 80–82
New Stanley Elementary School, xi, 73, 155,
  160, 161
  engaging students at, 83
  leadership at, 121–24, 131
  outside support and, 129
  removing failure at, 107–109, 189
  "replication" grant at, 83
  teachers and goal-setting at, 102
New York City:
  distinguished public schools in, 30, 31,
    54, 55
  Police Department, 107
New York Times, The, 31
New Zealand, 182–83
Next Century Schools, 24
  applications for grants, 99–100, 131–32
  bureaucracy and, 27–28
  communication and, 80–82
  emerging leaders at, 71
  establishment of, x–xv
  goal-setting at, 98–103
  leadership at, 120–29
  market forces and, 34, 44–45
  renewal of awards, 86–87
  "replication" grant from, 83
  selection of teachers at, 73–74
  technology and, 75–76
North Carolina School of Science and Mathematics (NCSSM), 55, 87, 223, 236
  selection of teachers at, 73

O'Melveny and Myers, 166
Optimization, 56–57
Orem High School, 162, 166, 247

284

Index

Ortega Elementary School, xi, 63, 71, 186
  parent-outreach at, 218–19
Outside pressure, 24
Outside services, 259–60
Outside support, 129–30

Paideia Proposal, The (Adler), 146–47
Parent education, 217–18
Parents, 197–226, 272
  business programs and, 219–21
  choice and, 43–44
  communication and, 80–82
  dissolution of family life, 201–202, 205–209
  educational role of, 202–205, 214–21
  financial support by, 225–26
  goal-setting and, 101
  leadership and, 123
  as obstacles to reform, 89–90
  outreach programs for, 214–19
  reinforcement of, by schools, 221–25
Park View Elementary School, xi, 28, 40, 48, 217
  extended-year concept at, 207, 221–22
Participants, teachers as, 154–57
Participation in society, 183, 184
Pathways program, 100
  Chelsea High School, 143–44, 150–52, 167
Patrick, Larry, 54
Paying for performance, 74, 167–69, 267
  productivity and, 234–35
Phi Delta Kappan, 8, 23
Physics teachers, 168
Pine Barrens school, 131–32
Piscataquis Community High School, xi, 28, 161
  computers at, 241–42
  described, 63–65, 68–69, 189
  distance-learning at, 236
  leadership at, 124–26, 131
  outside support and, 129
  teacher as coach at, 147–48
  team-building at, 155
"Political" model of schools, 26–27
Portfolios that demonstrate accomplishment, 104
Potomac Edison Power Company (Pepco), 66, 163, 248
Poulin, Raymond, Jr., 28, 124
Poverty, 5, 6, 71, 98
  choosing a school and, 48–49, 58–59, 84–85
  homelife and, 199–202, 205–209
  leadership and, 127–28
  parent outreach and, 218–19
  problems caused by, 230
  revival of public schools and, 269–70

school readiness and, 203
Preliminary Scholastic Aptitude Test (PSAT), 5–6
Pre-school PTAs, 203
Price, 33
Principals, 256, 257–60, 272
  customer requirements and, 49–50
  decentralization of power and, 259–60
  leadership by, 133, 136–38
  selection of, 70–71, 118–19, 257–58
  supply and demand and, 44
  tenure of, 257–58
Private schools, 32, 84
  characteristics of, 42, 86
Productivity, 227–50
  common denominators for, 243–44
  corporate, 233–35
  crisis in, 229–30, 249–50
  defined, 232–33
  increased, 233–50
  input-output problems, 230, 232–33
  investing to increase, 75–80
  labor, 234–35
  management and, 237–38, 246–47
  materials, 236–44
  money and, 76–77, 229–31
  plant and equipment, 235–36
  students as workers and, 239–40, 243, 244–45
  teachers and, 80, 246–47
  technology and, 75–76, 234–43, 247–48
  testing and, 109
  time on task and, 77–79
Professionals, 49–50
  teachers as, 144–45
Profit, 33
Proxies for achievement and competence, 182–83
"Public Attitudes Toward Public Education," xii
Public education:
  basic purposes of, 183–84, 239
  competitors of, for scarce resources, 230–31
  expenditures on, 229
  failure and, 86–87
  higher education compared to, 13–14
  inefficiency of, 234–38
  Mann and, 200, 210–11
  mass production concept of, 231–32, 242
  resistance to change, 3–4
  revival of, *see* Revival of American public schools
  technology and, *see* Technology
Public Interest, The (Moynihan), 197
Public-sector "investments," 38
"Pull-out" program, 208

285

Index

Index

Index